Love
Order & Chaos

LOVE
ORDER & CHAOS

The Universe as a Fractal
whose Strange Attractor is
Divine Love

A. J. Coriat

For as the heavens are higher than the earth,
so are my ways higher than your ways,
and my thoughts than your thoughts.

— Isaiah iv. 9

CONTENTS

INTRODUCTION

A science that does not evolve is a dead science. And a religion that is not in tune with reason and scientific evidence degenerates into superstition. We must not forget that not too long ago scientists believed that atoms were the smallest particles in the universe. And we should equally remember that, at one time, humans used to worship many gods. Thankfully, today, all legitimate religions are monotheistic. If there is only ONE God of the universe, who is the Father of all, many human beings wonder why God does not make His presence known in the world. They also question why He lets disorder and evil flourish? But is it God that is absent or is it rather that humans are no longer able to experience God's presence? And is it God that does not care or is it the fact that humans have abused their freewill and rationality?

When we superficially observe the world, although we do detect order on every scale, we do not see any direct evidence of God. The universe seems to be proceeding as of itself. For example, planets are rotating and revolving harmonically in accordance with the law of gravitation. On earth, plants, flowers and trees appear to be growing as of themselves in accordance with certain biological laws. Animals move, eat and survive as of themselves. Humans also seem to be struggling and living as of themselves. To all appearances, it seems that we have been abandoned in this material, cruel, uncertain and difficult world to fend for ourselves. But is this the reality?

Although humans tend to hold diverging views on almost every subject, there is at least one idea upon which they all seem to agree: the universe displays both order and chaos. When we study the natural world, we discover that most natural forms exhibit intricate levels of organization, symmetry and harmony. On the macrocosmic scale, the revolutions and rotations of galaxies, stars, planets and moons manifest a harmonic celestial dance that philosophers have appropriately called *the music of the spheres*. The earth itself consists of magnificent landscapes, green pastures, soaring mountains, rich forests, pristine oceans, unending beaches and peaceful sunsets. The mineral world gave birth to organized molecular structures such as pure diamonds, as well as the symmetrical and intelligent organization of the double helix DNA molecule. The vegetable kingdom is comprised of a rich variety of beautiful plants, majestic trees, charming flowers, nutritious vegetables and delicious fruits. Animals also tend to display beauty and order, as in the coordinated flight of geese, the gentle character of doves, deer and lambs and the colorful and artistic display of fish in the vastness of the ocean. On the human level, the graceful human form itself is the most intricate and intelligent organization on earth. Finally, the human heart and mind have the potential to experience the logic of rationality and the harmonies of love.

And yet, we seem to also experience disorder both in our outer world as well as within our inner realm of thoughts and affections. On earth, we regularly witness the devastation that earthquakes, storms, floods, fires, hurricanes and tornadoes inflict on the inhabitants of the land. The animal kingdom seems to be a harsh environment of survival of the fittest where fierce and malicious species such as jackals, wolves, alligators and snakes prey on gentle species such as lambs and deer. On the human level, selfish, cunning and mindless persons regularly prey on innocent victims. Inwardly, human beings also intermittently experience negative emotions such as fear, envy, anger, revenge and hatred as well as morbid thoughts such as worry, doubt, confusion, irrationality and insanity. Finally, on a global scale, we continue to experience conflict, violence, war, famine, poverty, perversity and disease. What is the driving cause behind order and chaos?

For thousands of years, philosophers and scientists have struggled to understand the wonders of the universe. And scientists, in the last few centuries, have discovered many laws that govern the material universe but they have yet to understand what caused the universe to spontaneously emerge and begin to evolve in an orderly fashion as of itself. Well, the answer to this fundamental and important question only begins to emerge when we realize that there must be an underlying Infinite Reality behind the world.

While studying complex and dynamical systems such as the weather, scientists have recently discovered a new theory which they have appropriately called *Chaos Theory*. They have found that, although complex or nonlinear systems tend to display chaotic behavior, as a whole, they are governed by an attractor that seems to restore order. And, although the parts of the universe are free to act, react and interact, and disorder seems to increase, such non-linear systems tend to eventually self-organize. In other words, there seems to be an underlying Reality that is restoring order and harmony everywhere. The physicist David Bohm even theorized that the universe embeds a generative order and that the parts are essentially governed by the whole.

It is also becoming increasingly evident that most of the laws of science may essentially be derived from a unifying principle. Newton's laws of motion and universal gravitation, Einstein's laws of relativity, Maxwell's laws of electromagnetism and Schrodinger's wave-function in quantum mechanics can all essentially be derived from *the principle of stationary action*.

Finally, the discovery of self-similarity and fractal geometry by Benoit Mandelbrot in 1975 seems to have stitched all these ideas together. The universe appears to be a fractal with a strange attractor. But chaotic fractals are not only mathematical and scientific; they are equally works of art. If the universe is such a fractal, it must not only be the result of scientific laws; it must also be a creative work of art. Beautiful human works of art have the capacity to imitate real life and evoke true thoughts and real emotions because they are both complex and coherent. Such works also tend to express the tension that exists between light and darkness, order and chaos, consonance and dissonance, truth and falsehood, good and evil. If artistic works are expressions of reality, the universe must be the ultimate work of art.

In the future, if we could discover the strange attractor of the universe, we would eventually understand the process, structure and purpose of universal reality. In fact, we do not have to wait for the future! More than two hundred years ago, the scientist Emanuel Swedenborg, while studying the complexity of the human brain and the cerebral cortex, was able to penetrate into the implicate order of the human mind and discover the essence of this strange attractor. While conscious in the spiritual world, Swedenborg detected that the universe was generated, maintained, sustained and periodically restored by Divine Love. This was the universe's fractal generator and strange attractor. He equally found that disorder in the world stemmed from the disorder in the human mind and heart, a consequence of man's spiritual downfall. In this book, we are going to discover how mathematics, fractal geometry and Chaos Theory seem to corroborate what Swedenborg already discovered more than two hundred years ago. The universe is an eternal work of art, the artist is God, and the means by which this work of art is generated, re=formed and re-generated is Divine Love.

Love
Order & Chaos

I
BEAUTY

Chapter 1
MATHEMATICAL BEAUTY:

HARMONY

Most mathematicians agree that mathematics reflects Beauty or Truth. But they have yet to agree on what this Truth is. Since numbers and order are related, scientists regularly use mathematics to model the order, structure or form of the universe. For example, geometry is the study of forms in space. And calculus is widely utilized to determine how things change in time. But the other reason mathematics is useful is because it is not limited to physical space. The space of mathematics is infinite. Mathematical space is conceptual space. Hence, mathematics is also able to give us information about what is beyond our physical world; it enables us to explore the realm of mind and ideas.

Our physical body is in physical space where objects

exist but our mind must be in conceptual space where concepts or ideas subsist. In fact, idealist philosophers, such as Plato, believed that the physical universe was derived from a world of *Platonic Ideas*. But, if this world of ideas is real, it should not only consist of forms; it should also need to be substantial. As Swedenborg discovered, anything real must consist of *Substance, Form and Process* because these three essential and discrete categories are always linked like *End, Cause and Effect*.

We know that our physical and actual world is real because it consists of objects whose forms we can see with our eyes and whose substances we can touch with our hands. And, if we assume that there is a realm beyond this physical world and this other world is real, we should equally be able to perceive its forms and touch its substances. We have deduced that the forms of this other realm are concepts or ideas that we can perceive with our mind. Mathematics cannot help us experience the substance of these ideas but it can assist us in discovering their form or structure.

The only thing we know for sure is that, if God is real or even Reality itself, He should consist of *Substance, Form and Process*. And the only reason the universe must necessarily exist is because it must be part of God's process. We already know very much about God's process from the discoveries of natural science. But what can mathematics tell us about Heaven or God's substance and form? In physics, we know that mass is equivalent to energy. Therefore, all substances in the physical universe are essentially energy. This energy is always in some physical form and it acts according to physical laws.

Now, we are assuming that what is beyond the quantum world is also real. And, if it is real, it must consist of some kind of non-physical energy and this energy must be in some form. And, if God is Reality itself or the INFINITE ONE from which everything proceeds, He must consist of some kind of transcendental energy. This energy must be in some kind of non-physical form. And we are saying that this form is a conceptual form or an Idea. Let us discover if mathematics can tell us something about the INFINITE ONE.

In mathematics, we know that there are several species of numbers. For example, 1 is a Natural number or integer. It is a whole or quantum number. Natural numbers such as ...-3, -2, -1, 0, +1, +2, +3.... are discrete. Rational numbers are numbers that can be expressed as fractions or ratios. The decimal expansion of a Rational Number either terminates or repeats. For example,

$$1/2 = 0.5$$

$$1/3 = 0.333333333333333333333333333\cdots$$

$$1/7 = 0.142857\ 142857\ 142857\ 142857\ldots$$

An Irrational number is a number that cannot be expressed as a fraction. For example, $\sqrt{2}$ cannot be described as a fraction and its decimal expansion does not repeat:

$$\sqrt{2} = 1.41421356237309504880168872420969 8078\ldots\ldots$$

Irrational numbers such as $\sqrt{2}$ are not discrete, static or finite like the Natural numbers or repeating like the Rational Numbers. And, although $\sqrt{2}$ cannot be described as a fraction, it can be expressed as a continued fraction:

$$\sqrt{2} = 1 + \cfrac{1}{2 + \cfrac{1}{2 + \cfrac{1}{2 + \cfrac{1}{2 + \ddots}}}}$$

This continued fraction seems to be self-similar or fractal. In fact, Irrational numbers are not really irrational or disordered. We can instead describe them as *infinitely rational*, dynamic or infinitely ALIVE. And, moreover, conceptual space is not dead; it is a space that is infinitely dynamic and alive.

Together, the Rational and Irrational numbers form the Real numbers or all the points on a line. Ratios describe the relationship between two numbers. Thus, the Real numbers must describe how ideas are related in mathematical or conceptual space. And, if conceptual space is ONE and INFINITE, numbers must also describe how finite ideas are related to the idea of God or the INFINITE ONE. Mathematics is useful because it can tell us how things are not only related in physical space and time but also

how they are related to conceptual space and the INFI-
NITE ONE.

In mathematics, numbers can be used to represent
quantity. For example, 3 is more than 2. Why? Well, we are
told that

$$2 = 1 + 1$$
$$3 = 1 + 1 + 1$$

Thus, all numbers are really derived from 1. Numbers can
also be used to determine order or organization, as in the
order of points on a line (Fig. 1.1). In this case, 2 comes after 1 and 3 comes after 2. Why? Well, we are told that this
is how numbers are ordered on the WHOLE infinite line.
In fact, this regimented sequence is just an arbitrary order. And we do not really know how points or Real numbers are ordered on the infinite line! We just know that
there are an infinite number of points or Real numbers on
an infinite line.

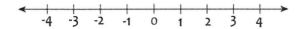

Fig. 1.1. Numbers as Points on an Infinite Line

Now, the mathematician Georg Cantor, while studying
infinity, proved mathematically that there as many points
or Real numbers on an infinite line, plane or solid as there
are on any finite line, plane or solid. In both cases, the
number of points is infinite. Therefore, instead of using an
infinite line, we can use a finite line, plane or space to rep-

resent the Absolute One of mathematical or conceptual space (Fig 1.2). But what about the negative numbers, where do they originate? Well, we are told that the square root of absolute 1 is

$$\sqrt{1} = +1 \text{ or } -1$$

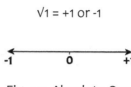

Fig. 1.2. Absolute One

It seems that by taking the root of absolute 1, we are discovering what is within conceptual space. This segment is comprised of an infinity of Real numbers. And the polarity of numbers, positive or negative is simply indicating direction in conceptual space. We know that when we take the square root of an absolute Real number, we obtain a Real number. For example, $\sqrt{4} = +2$ or -2. But what happens when we take the square root of a negative number such as $\sqrt{-4}$? We do obtain another number but this number is not Real; it is Imaginary. By taking the square root of negative numbers, mathematicians have discovered another mathematical realm: the realm of Imaginary numbers. A Complex number consists of a real and an imaginary part or a + bi, where a and b are Real numbers and $i = \sqrt{-1}$ is an Imaginary number. Complex numbers can be represented on a complex plane with the horizontal axis as the Real numbers and the vertical axis as the Imaginary numbers (Fig 1.3) . It seems that, by taking the roots of Absolute One, we are unraveling more and more dimensions.

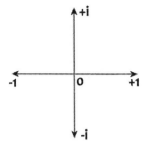

Fig. 1. 3. The Complex Plane

Is there any way to know how numbers are related in the complexity of the complex plane of the Absolute One? Strangely enough, the answer is YES. The mathematician Leonard Euler discovered the most important formula in mathematics: Euler's Formula. And this formula can be represented geometrically:

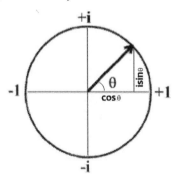

$$e^{i\theta} = \cos\theta + i\sin\theta$$

Fig. 1.4. Euler's Formula

This circle is a representation of WHOLENESS or how ideas are related in the conceptual space of absolute 1. Therefore, we should not believe that this circle is finite. Remember, we are in mathematical or conceptual space, not physical space. We would like to understand how concepts are related within the ONE from which all ideas or forms proceed. We should not also erroneously believe that this circle is static. No, it is infinitely dynamic and ALIVE. It represents LIFE within the INFINITE ONE. The numbers i, e and π are all alive. The circle itself consists of 2π; it represents all the possible locations or points the radius $e^{i\theta}$ can occupy. In other words, 2π represents all the possibilities within the 1. What does 0 represent? Conventionally, we think of zero as nothing. However, here, zero represents equilibrium within the Absolute One. At $\Theta = 0$, $e^{i\theta} = e^0 = 1$. In figure 1.5, we have represented this circle as the Absolute Sun in conceptual space from which all possibilities proceed.

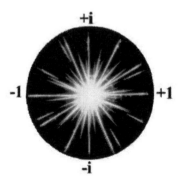

Fig. 1.5. The Absolute Sun in Conceptual Space

Here, we discover that a number, any species of number, is just a symbol for how things or concepts are related in mathematical or conceptual space. Can we move beyond the complex plane? The Irish mathematician William Rowan Hamilton wondered if he could extend these numbers beyond the complex plane. He was constantly thinking and pondering about this problem without success. However, on the 16th of October, 1843, as he walked near Bloome bridge in Dublin, the answer came to him (Fig. 1.6). A quaternion consists of a real and three imaginary parts, a + bi + cj + dk. And Hamilton discovered on that very day that these Imaginary numbers are related in this way:

$$i^2 = j^2 = k^2 = ijk = -1$$

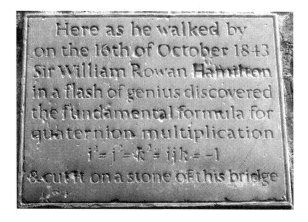

Fig. 1.6. Plaque on Bloome Bridge, Dublin, Ireland

We can also notice that quaternions are noncommutative. For example, ij is not equal to ji. ij = -k and ji = k. The multiplication table of quaternions is shown below:

	1	i	j	k
1	1	i	j	k
i	i	-1	k	-j
j	j	-k	-1	i
k	k	j	-i	-1

Table 1.1. Quaternion Multiplication Table

Complex numbers and quaternions have many uses in mathematics and science. But how do they relate to our present study? Quaternions describe how things rotate or spin in the universe. For example, when we multiply +1 by i, we have rotated by 90 degrees. Quaternions are spinors. i causes spin. Multiplication by i moves the radius by 90 degrees or $\pi/2$. +1 times i equals +i, +i times i equal -1, -1 times i equals -i and so on, around and around. And we know that in the physical universe celestial objects, such as planets, are also spinning and revolving. Elementary particles, such as electrons, are equally spinning perpetually. But it seems that this perpetual motion or spin originates in mathematical or conceptual space. Quaternions, themselves, are constants that have no units; they have no physical mass, no charge and no time. But they have spin. Quaternions subsist in mathematical or conceptual space. In our case, we are equally assuming that this conceptual space is real, substantial and energetic. And we are trying to discover how concepts are related in this conceptual space.

In mathematical symbols, God is absolute 1. But, if God is also infinite, this constant 1 must contain infinite realities within itself. These infinite realities must equally be infinitely related to each other and to the Infinite One. And even though the universe is generated from 1, 1 remains constant or 1. God is transcendent because He remains true to Himself or ONE. But He must be equally immanent because the whole universe is generated, maintained and restored from His substance or energy. This energy must be infinite, dynamic and ALIVE. God must be LIFE itself.

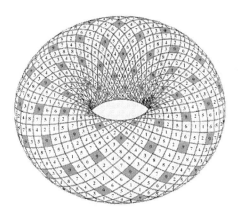

Fig. 1.7. Vortex-based Mathematics (Marko Rodin)

The multiplication table 1.1 tells us how quaternions interact in conceptual space. This table can be mapped in three dimensions to show how quaternions are related in higher dimensions (Fig. 1.7). Marko Rodin discovered that the Natural, whole or quantum numbers are related vortically. He called this *voxtex-based mathematics*. But Willie Johnson Jr., in his book *Po, Pi, Phi and Psi (The ijk's of Vortex Mathematics)*, demonstrates that this vorticity is equivalent to the relationship and interaction between quaternions. And we have discovered that quaternions within the Absolute One are related in this way:

$$i^2 = j^2 = k^2 = ijk = -1$$

But we also know that when $\theta = \pi$,

$$e^{i\pi} = -1$$

Therefore,

$$e^{i\pi} = i^2 = j^2 = k^2 = ijk = -1$$

Now, e and π are not just Irrational numbers; they are also Transcendental numbers. In mathematics, a Transcendental number is defined as *a real or complex number that is not algebraic or a root of a non-zero polynomial equation with rational coefficients*. We do not really need to understand what this means. What is important for us to understand is that a Transcendental number is also a number that is infinitely ALIVE, but alive in a way that transcends other numbers. In this equation, we have three mathematical constants, e, π and i interacting with each other and equal to -1. Over the last few centuries, many mathematicians already recognized the beauty of this equation because it incorporated most of nature's fundamental constants. However, in his amazing book, *The Sagitta Key*, Willie Johnson Jr. demonstrates how this equation is the most powerful equation in mathematics, physics and chemistry. Essentially, it is the key to understanding the whole universe.

We know that π is Irrational and Transcendental. Therefore, it can also be described as an infinite continued series:

$$\pi = \frac{4}{1} - \frac{4}{3} + \frac{4}{5} - \frac{4}{7} + \frac{4}{9} - \cdots$$

Once again, from this infinite series, we notice that π is infinitely alive; it is expanding and contracting (or vibrating) infinitely.

What about the mysterious number e?

e = 2.7182818284590452353602874713........

We notice that e is also Irrational and Transcendental. And, if 2π represents a circle, e represents the Natural logarithmic spiral. Now, in mathematics, the logarithm of a number is the exponent to which a base number must be raised to obtain that number. Any number can be used as a base. For example, computer science utilizes the base number 2. However, it seems that the universe is being generated using the base or quantum number e because the Natural logarithmic spiral is prevalent in nature. This spiral is a self-similar function or fractal. And it has been called *spira mirabilis* or *marvelous spiral* because it has many miraculous properties. But its most important property is that it cannot be changed or transformed. It remains true to itself. Hence, it is the only function in mathematics that equals its derivative and integral.

$$de^{i\theta} / d\Theta = e^{i\theta}$$

$$\int e^{i\theta} = e^{i\theta}$$

This is really an astounding property when we think about it because everything in the universe involves, evolves and transforms with time. But the natural logarithmic spiral itself cannot and does not change. We then see that this equation must also be the source of calculus or changes in state. But this equation never changes; it remains constant, perpetual and eternal.

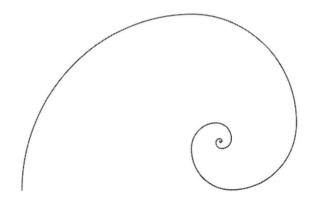

Fig 1.8. Natural Logarithmic Spiral

Although $e^{i\theta}$ does not change, we can nevertheless see that it is evolving infinitely. Hence, we can conclude that it is causing involution and evolution from conceptual space. This whole equation, which consists of living constants, must be driving or propelling the whole universe to spin, involve and evolve from conceptual space; it is generating the fractal of the universe. But conceptual space and physical space are discrete and separate. The forms and substances of the universe may be spinning, involving, evolving and transforming but these constants remain constant, eternal and infinitely alive.

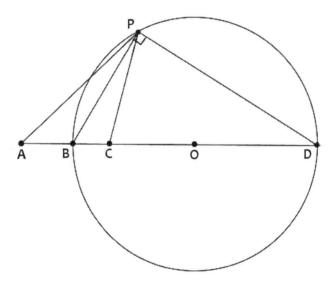

Fig. 1.9. Harmonic Cross-ratio

Now that we have determined what e, π, and i represent, we should try to discover if there are other constants in conceptual space that are equal to $e^{i\pi}$ or -1. For example, in projective geometry, the harmonic cross-ratio is equal to -1. The cross-ratio is the ratio between internal and external division in projective space. In projective geometry, the cross-ratio is one of the few properties that are invariant under projective transformation. In figure 1.9, we can see four points projected from the source point P. In projective space, the cross-ratio can have any value. However, when the cross-ratio is equal to -1, the points C and D are called *harmonic conjugates* and the cross-ratio is said to be *harmonic*:

Harmonic Cross-ratio = $(CA/CB)/(DA/DB)$ = -1 = $e^{i\pi}$

Another constant that we find profusely in nature is phi, φ or the Golden Ratio. This is the harmonic ratio between the whole and its parts. When the ratio of a whole line to its larger part is equal to the ratio of its larger part to its smaller part, the line is divided or related according to the Golden Ratio or φ,

Fig. 1.10. The Golden Ratio

$\varphi = (a+b)/a = a/b = 1.6180339887....$

Although φ is not a Transcendental number, it is an Irrational number that also has many miraculous properties. For example,

$$\varphi = \sqrt{1 + \sqrt{1 + \sqrt{1 + \sqrt{1 + \cdots}}}}$$

$$\varphi = 1 + \cfrac{1}{1 + \cfrac{1}{1 + \cfrac{1}{1 + \cdots}}}$$

$$1/\varphi = \varphi - 1$$
$$\varphi^2 = \varphi + 1$$

This equally means that

$$\varphi - \varphi^2 = -1 = e^{i\pi}.$$

A Golden Spiral is a logarithmic spiral with a growth factor of φ.

Now, what do all these constants have in common? They all seem to be expressions of HARMONY in conceptual space. The only way God's substance or energy can be both 1 and infinite is by being infinitely harmonized. Why? Since God is Infinite, He must embed all the infinite complexity or chaos of conceptual space within Himself. But, if God is also One or in harmony with Himself, all these concepts or realities must be harmonically related to each other and to God. In God or the Infinite One, Infinity represents infinite complexity or Chaos and Oneness or unity represents Order. Chaos is Freedom and Order is Law. But, in God, Chaos and Order or Freedom and Law must be infinitely harmonized. The Infinite One contains infinite realities but these realities are infinitely and harmonically organized.

Our own human mind finds it difficult to reconcile Order and Chaos. This is probably because our mind is finite while God's mind is infinite. Now, although our mind is finite, it is unbounded. This means that our mind can continue to evolve, although it will never reach the mind of God. There is no doubt that the universe is infinitely complex or chaotic but it is equally true that there is an underlying Order on every level. Most scientists would be willing to agree that this is true of physical, chemical or even biological processes. However, they still question where physical laws originate. We are claiming that the laws of physical space originate from the laws of conceptual space, the mind of God or the Infinite One.

The Infinite One or God generates the universe from the infinite harmony of His substance (energy) in conceptual space. The physicist David Bohm postulated that the universe consists of an implicate and an explicate order. The explicate order is the physical realm of matter, space and time. And the generative or implicate order is the holomovement embedded within every part of the universe. This movement of the whole is continually unfolding and enfolding or involving and evolving. As far as we are concerned, the implicate order must be the harmonic order of conceptual space that we are presently exploring. This equation is essentially a conceptual gyroscope that is perpetually generating, maintaining, sustaining and restoring the universe. In fact, Willie Johnson Jr. was able to produce a *Gyroscopic Force Theory* of the universe from this equation. However, we are especially interested in how this equation relates to what is happening in the conceptual space or the Heaven of our mind.

Fig. 1.11. Gyroscope

Now, if Heaven is real, it should not only have form; it should also have substance or energy. What is the substance or energy of this conceptual gyroscope by which the INFINITE ONE generates the universe? Mathematically or conceptually, this equation consists of spinors in conceptual space. Physically, a gyroscope has a heavy rotor that is in constant circular motion (Fig. 1.11). We may then assume that this conceptual gyroscope must be God's will. It is a kind of motion or impetus that drives or propels the whole universe. It cannot be a physical motion because it resides in conceptual space. Therefore, we could call it an *e-motion*. God's will, energy or substance must be *harmonic e-motion* or Divine Love. And God's mind, form or structure must be *harmonic form* or Divine Truth. Heaven must consist of harmonic emotions and concepts. Plato was right but not completely! In order to be real his Ideal or *Platonic Forms* need to be substantial or energetic. And we now discover that their substance or energy is none other than Divine Love or Harmonic E-motion.

Divine Love is an emotional and conceptual gyroscope that generates, sustains, maintains and restores the universe. We know that physical gyroscopes are used to maintain stability and equilibrium in physical systems. Similarly, Divine Love not only generates and propels all things; it also maintains equilibrium, stability and harmony in conceptual as well as in physical space. All the laws of the universe can be derived from the gyroscopic action of Divine Love. If we understood how the gyroscope of Divine Love works, we would understand how everything functions in the universe.

Divine Love is a self-existent, eternal and perpetual harmonic e-motion or energy that is driving the whole universe. And beyond the quaternions, there must be other hypernumbers and more inner dimensions such as octonions and sedenions because conceptual space is infinite. We can continue to approach the Absolute One or get closer to God but we can never reach Him. This is because our mind is finite and unbounded while God is Infinite. For example, we discovered that by taking the square root of Absolute One, we obtain +1 and -1. And, by taking the square root of -1, we obtain a whole other realm of Imaginary numbers. Therefore, $\sqrt{+1}$ is not equivalent to $\sqrt{1}$ or the root of Absolute One. $\sqrt{0}$ is also not equivalent to 0. In fact, Charles Muses discovered that $\sqrt{+1}$ and $\sqrt{0}$ are hypernumbers or whole other realms within Absolute One.

	e_0	e_1	e_2	e_3	e_4	e_5	e_6	e_7
e_0	e_0	e_1	e_2	e_3	e_4	e_5	e_6	e_7
e_1	e_1	$-e_0$	e_3	$-e_2$	e_5	$-e_4$	$-e_7$	e_6
e_2	e_2	$-e_3$	$-e_0$	e_1	e_6	e_7	$-e_4$	$-e_5$
e_3	e_3	e_2	$-e_1$	$-e_0$	e_7	$-e_6$	e_5	$-e_4$
e_4	e_4	$-e_5$	$-e_6$	$-e_7$	$-e_0$	e_1	e_2	e_3
e_5	e_5	e_4	$-e_7$	e_6	$-e_1$	$-e_0$	$-e_3$	e_2
e_6	e_6	e_7	e_4	$-e_5$	$-e_2$	e_3	$-e_0$	$-e_1$
e_7	e_7	$-e_6$	e_5	e_4	$-e_3$	$-e_2$	e_1	$-e_0$

Table 1.2. Multiplication Table of Octonions

In this book, we are going to confine our understanding of Love to quaternions and Euler's formula and not delve into the mathematics of octonions, sedenions or other hypernumbers because the subject is too complex. However, if we think that the multiplication table of quaternions is complex, we have not seen the multiplication tables of octonions and sedenions (Table 1.2). These mathematical operations and relationships are infinitely complex because they represent the self-existent flow of Love and the infinitely complex and coherent relationship that exists in reality between Love and Truth. Such infinite complexity is also present in the curves and inflections of the Hebrew alphabet because the Bible is the Word of God or Divine Truth. Swedenborg also discovered that numbers in Heaven represent the mysteries of Divine Love and Wisdom like the letters and words of the Bible:

> I have also seen writings from heaven made up of mere numbers set down in order and in a series, just as in writings made up of letters and words; and I have been taught that this writing is from the inmost heaven, and that their heavenly writing, when the thought from it flows down, is set forth before the angels of the lower heavens in numbers, and that this numerical writing likewise involves arcana, some of which can neither be comprehended by thought nor expressed by words. For all numbers correspond, and have a meaning, the same as words do, in accordance with the correspondence; yet with the difference that in numbers generals are involved, and in words particulars; and as one general involves innumerable particulars, so more arcana are involved in numerical writing than in literal writing. (Swedenborg, Emanuel, Heaven and Hell (1758), #263, translated by John C. Ager, 1900.)

The quaternions interact with each other like involving and evolving spirals or vortices (Fig. 1.12). But the sum or integral of this interaction is equilibrium or harmony. Divine Love is HARMONIC E-MOTION (Fig. 1.13). And involution and evolution must be harmonic conjugates. Quaternions are conjugates. Most elementary particles are also conjugates because they are being generated by Love from conceptual space. Daniel Winter has discovered that the waves of the universe can only interfere constructively when they interfere fractally according to the Golden Ratio. In his book, *Fractal Conjugate Space and Time*, he provides convincing evidence of this Golden Ratio interference on all levels of the universe. This is in agreement with what we previously discovered concerning the constants of the universe.

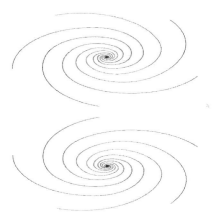

Fig. 1.12. Involution and Evolution

By means of these three essential aspects of Divine Love (involution, evolution, and realization) we should be able to understand how the fractal of the universe is generated, maintained and restored by the Divine Love of God or the INFINITE ONE. Understanding how quater-

nions behave can also shed light on how the physical universe was generated from conceptual space. For example, scientists have speculated that the universe emerged
from a gravitational singularity by means of a Big Bang.
They believe the universe expanded from a hot and dense
state of energy which eventually crystallized into subatomic particles and then into atoms such as Hydrogen.
And then giant clouds of Hydrogen condensed through
gravity to form stars and galaxies. This is known as the *Big
Bang theory.* But, from what we have previously discussed, we can readily conclude that the universe could
only have involved from God's energy or Divine Love and
it continues to be maintained and restored by the strange
attractor of Love.

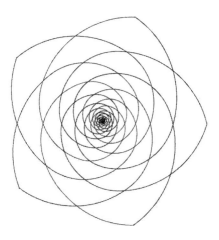

Fig. 1.13. Harmonic E-motion or Divine Love

Many scientists also continue to believe that life and intelligence on earth emerged by chance or accident. Darwin believed that species evolved through random genetic mutation and the species that were most fit to survive and adapt to their environment tended to thrive and multiply while the rest became extinct. Thus, according to Darwin, human beings evolved into existence because those species that were cunning (or intelligent) in finding ways to survive in the world were able to procreate and multiply. However, from what we have discovered so far, we can already conclude that Intelligence (Truth) and Love were already present within the Infinite One or God before the material world was generated by the fractal generator of Love. We can equally conjecture that all created beings involved from Divine Love and must be evolving or re-turning to Divine Love. This would explain why human beings have evolved a mind to understand concepts and a will to love. Our brain and our mind are discrete and separate but they are related by *correspondence*. Our brain is in physical space while our mind is in conceptual space. Quaternions are in the conceptual space of our mind while electrons and protons are in the physical space of our brain. Our brain is physically real because it consists of physical energy but our mind is equally real because it consists of mental and emotional energy.

Before Chaos Theory, scientists believed that all things were decaying with time. This is because they thought that time was a linear or an irreversible process from order to disorder. And some physicists even predicted the heat death of the universe. It is true that all things are decaying with time or moving from order to disorder. But, from Chaos theory, we now know that time is not linear and order can also emerge from disorder. This is even easier to see from our pictures of involution and evolution (Fig. 1.12). Involution is the process from order to disorder but, when this disorder reaches its critical maximum, order emerges once again from disorder. This is caused by the attractor of Divine Love. In the physical universe, we can witness this process everywhere: birth, growth, decay, death, birth, growth ... etc. This is how eternal life manifests in the physical world. The death or end of any process contains the seed or beginning of a new process.

Fig. 1.14. Yin-Yang Symbol

This relationship between order and disorder is also well-illustrated by the Yin-Yang symbol of Taoism (Fig. 1.14). In this symbol, we are able to discern that opposites are in reality complementary or conjugates and they give rise to each other. The symbol consists of Light and Dark areas. But we also notice that the dark area contains the seed of light. And, when the dark area or disorder reaches its maximum, light or order is born again and begins to grow until it also reaches its maximum. Then things start to deteriorate again and the cycle repeats. However, what we should also remember is that all these processes are kept in equilibrium by the gyroscope of Divine Love. This is probably why the Tao is translated as the *Way of Harmony*. We can also readily notice that this symbol is a cross-section of a torus or a four-dimensional sphere. And we have also seen that the torus or vortex represents the relationship between quaternions.

In God (Infinite Oneness), Chaos (Infinite Complexity) is harmonized with Order (Infinite Unity). Infinite complexity is FREEDOM and Infinite unity is LAW. God is Divine Love (Freedom) and Divine Truth (Law). And, in God, Love and Truth are infinitely harmonized. However, the universe manifests Order and Disorder because all the parts of the universe are relatively Free to act, react and interact. But these parts and their actions, reactions and interactions are interrelated and regulated by Divine Order or Law.

Fig. 1.15. A Seesaw and its Fulcrum

We can also picture this relationship between the parts and the whole as a seesaw, which is an extremely simplified model of the universe (Fig. 1.15). First, we notice that a seesaw consists of two parts that can freely move or act, react and interact. But these two parts are interconnected, related and stabilized by means of a fulcrum. The fulcrum represents the conceptual gyroscope of Divine

Love. The fulcrum and the parts are interconnected. Yet, no matter how much the parts freely move, act and react, they can never disturb the fulcrum. And any free action on one side is automatically balanced by a reaction on the opposite side due to the fulcrum. This is the Law. Of course, in the universe, this is more difficult to perceive because the number of parts is endless and these parts appear to be separate, although they are interconnected by Love.

Involution and evolution are synonymous with David Bohm's holomovement of unfoldment and enfoldment. This holomovement is ubiquitous throughout the universe. All things are unfolding and enfolding. Unfoldment is a movement from the conceptual space of Love into the world of matter. And enfoldment is a return to Love. As our life unfolds in time, we are also recording memories within our mind and this intelligence is encoded in our DNA for future generations. Through the memories of all existential beings, the collective energy field of the universe becomes increasingly complex and intelligent. And these two movements are always stabilized or balanced by the gyroscope of Love.

All things in the universe are also growing or involving like fractals because Divine Love or Harmonic E-motion is a fractal generator. The universe appears to consist of parts that are interacting with each other. But, if these parts are perpetually being generated from Divine Love and re-turning to Divine Love, they must all be interrelated by Divine Love. Divine Love is the whole. And the parts of the universe must be generated, maintained, governed, sustained and restored by the whole. The universe is a dynamic, complex and chaotic system because all parts are interrelated and interacting with each other and the whole. And, since the universe is a chaotic system, it must be self-similar. This essentially means that all beings are self-similar images of Divine Love. And the whole universe must be a reflected image of Divine Love.

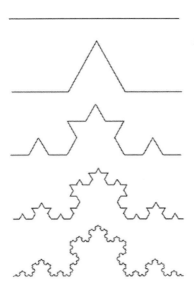

Fig. 1.16. The Koch Curve

If the universe is a fractal, it would be wise to study the geometry of fractals. This all started when Benoit Mandelbrot wished to determine the real or exact length of the coastline of Britain. We know that most lengths in the physical world are not straight like in the mathematical world. In fact, most things in the natural world are curved, jagged or crooked. For example, landscapes on earth consist of mountains and valleys. And, as we zoom in, or look closer, we find smaller peaks and valleys. For example, when we measure a coastline, if we use a fairly long measuring stick, we obtain an approximate and finite length. However, what if we use a shorter measuring stick? We must then include all the smaller and smaller lengths. And the smaller the measuring stick is, the longer the coastline becomes. Now, what if we continue to add all the smaller lengths all the way down to the atomic level and beyond? Like Mandelbrot, we would in fact discover that the coastline is infinitely long. And, since this coastline is not linear, it is also not one-dimensional. It has a dimension between 1 and 2. Mandelbrot calls these *fractal dimensions*. In fact, fractal dimensions are a measure of complexity. This is clearer to understand from seeing the Koch curve in figure 1.16.

In order to generate the Koch curve or fractal, we start the process with one angular peak. This is the first iteration of the Koch curve. Then, by repeating the process, with every subsequent iteration we obtain a curve that is self-similar. In this fractal curve, every part of the curve is similar to the whole curve. If we assume that the length of the initial line is 1, the length becomes longer and longer (1, 4/3, 16/9, 64/27...). The Koch curve lies somewhere between a one-dimensional line and a 2-D plane. Its fractal dimension is 1.26. We may have also noticed that this is how trees grow in nature (Fig 1.17). Every branch on any level of a tree is similar to the whole tree. The roots are also growing fractally and adapting to the environment of the soil in order to assimilate as much food and water from the earth as possible. What is important to under-stand about fractal growth is that it is not a linear process. In fact, in mathematics, fractals are generated by means of a feedback equation. For example, the Mandelbrot set (Fig. 1.19) is generated from the following equation:

$$Z_{n+1} = Z_n^2 + C, \text{ where Z is a complex number}$$

Fig. 1.17. Fractal Tree

What this means is that to produce the next iteration of a fractal, we must use the previous iteration. This is why a tree embeds or enfolds all its history within itself. Its frac-tal growth represents how it has evolved and adapted to the climatic changes of its uncertain environment. Biolo-gists are even able to determine a tree's age by examining the concentric rings of its trunk (Fig. 1.18). But, in fact, the tree's history is enfolded within its seed. In the case of a fruit tree, these seeds are in its fruits. The DNA within these seeds contains the intelligence that the tree has accumulated during its growth and existence. And this intelligence is past on to future generations. Seeds are not inert because they consist of DNA vortices of information and life. When they are planted in the soil, the process of duplication is activated by the fractal generator of Love and a new tree begins to unfold and enfold fractally.

Fig. 1.18. Concentric Rings in Tree Trunk

Although the fractal growth of a human being is much more complex, it is still very similar to the growth of a tree. We start out as a living cell consisting of millions of helices of DNA. But this cell equally embeds or enfolds the history of the whole universe, the involution and evolution of planets, stars and galaxies. This history also includes the memory of the whole evolution of mineral, vegetable, animal and human life on earth. This information is encoded in the human genome or blueprint of our DNA. Specifically, our DNA also incorporates the history of our own human ancestry, the history of our parents and grandparents. Physically, our human digestive, circulatory and nervous systems also grow fractally. The various vessels and nerve fibers of the human anatomy unfold fractally like the branches of a tree. The psychology of our mind and will must also be chaotic and fractal. This is why we may periodically experience confusion or chaos within our mind and negative emotions within our heart. But we equally have the potential to reason intelligently and to experience the inner freedom and harmony of Love.

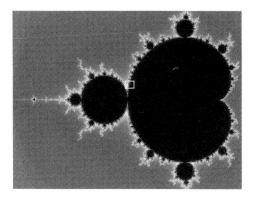

Fig. 1.19. The Mandelbrot Set

Therefore, the other important reason we should study fractal geometry is because fractals are able to reconcile Order (unity) and Chaos (complexity). And we know that the universe does seem to display both order and disorder. The universe is a dynamical system because

it consists of an endless number of parts that are interacting with each other as well as with the whole. And this
whole non-linear system is evolving with time. However, it
is not evolving randomly but in accordance with certain
Laws of Order. The parts of the universe are also Free to
interact with each other but this interaction is regulated
by Law. Therefore, Order and Chaos as well as Law and
Freedom must be linked in some way. In fact, we discovered that, in Divine Love, Chaos and Order were infinitely
harmonized. This is what Chaos theory also stipulates.

Fig. 1.20. Zoom into Mandelbrot set

Chaos theory was born when scientists attempted to
understand and forecast the weather. The weather is difficult to predict because it consists of a great number of
parts that are interacting with each other and the whole
system is evolving and feeding back upon itself over time.
Thus even a small perturbation in a remote part of the
system can cause a great disturbance within the whole.
Scientists have equally found that, although the weather
may become chaotic during certain periods, it still seems

to be governed by underlying laws of order. Hence, after periods of disorder such as storms, hurricanes and tornadoes, order within the natural atmosphere is reestablished. In other words, they no longer believe that dynamical systems are just degenerating or decaying with time. When this disorder reaches its maximum critical point, they have noticed that these systems tend to self-organize. This equally means that time is nonlinear and order can emerge from disorder.

A chaotic and fractal system like the weather seems to embed what scientists call an *attractor*. The attractor is the form to which the dynamical system returns as it evolves over time. For example, the attractor of the Mandelbrot set is shown in figure 1.19. This form reappears after a certain number of iterations. Thus, as we zoom into deeper and deeper levels of this fractal, we discover all kinds of beautiful forms involving and evolving. But, periodically, we see this form reappear again and again (Fig. 1.20).

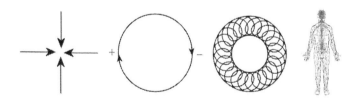

Fig. 1.21. Fixed Point, Cycle, Torus and Strange Attractors

Depending on the type of dynamical system, there are different kinds of attractors. For example, a simple system has an attractor that does not move or a *fixed point attractor.* A dynamical system that cycles periodically over the same state has what is called a *limit cycle attractor.* If there is more than one frequency involved and these frequencies are related irrationally, the dynamical system will be regulated by a *torus attractor.* Finally , a chaotic, unbounded and complex system such as the whole universe tends to have a very complex, detailed or *strange attractor* (Fig. 1.21).

As a result of everything we have discovered so far, we can now speculate that the whole universe must be a fractal and this fractal is being generated by the infinitely complex and harmonic fractal generator of Divine Love from conceptual space. Our mind may not be able to conceive such a fractal form. However, from the forms that have already been fractally generated through billions and billions of years of involution and evolution, we should be able to predict what this universal form could be. God is generating the whole universe by Divine Love but He remains true to Himself or transcendent. In such a universe, everything should be a self-similar image of Divine Love. And, as the universe involves and evolves, it should become an increasingly perfect image of God or Divine Love.

At this point, many of us may wonder: how could Emanuel Swedenborg, a man who lived in the eighteenth century and was interested in the meaning of the Bible, help us in our task and what would he know about fractal geometry and Chaos Theory? And the answer is simple. If Truth is universal, omnipresent and eternal, it should transcend time and space. Swedenborg spent his entire life searching for Truth or Reality. Like most scientists, he began this quest by studying the natural world of sensual experience. But he soon realized that the human mind did not subsist in natural space but in a spiritual space that was discrete and separate. And yet, these two spaces were linked through *correspondence*. Swedenborg may have existed in the physical world of the eighteenth century but his mind was able to perceive the nature of Reality because he was conscious in conceptual space. In fact, he understood the relationship between Order (unity) and Chaos (complexity) long before anyone else:

> *Everyone who traces effects back to their causes may know that the consistence of all things depends on order; and that there are many kinds of order, general and particular; and that there is one order which is the most universal of all, and on which depends the general and particular kinds in connected series; also that this most universal order enters into all the others as the essence itself into its forms, and that thus and not otherwise do they make one. It is this unity that effects the preservation of the whole, which would otherwise fall asunder, and relapse not only into primal chaos, but into nothing.* (Swedenborg, Emanuel, *True Christian Religion* (1770), #679, translated by John C. Ager, 1970)

> *Before anything is reduced into a state of order, it is most usual that things should be reduced into a confused mass, or chaos as it were, so that those which do not well cohere together may be separated, and when they are separated, then the Lord disposes*

them into order. This process may be compared with what takes place in nature, where all things in general and singly are first reduced to a confused mass, before being disposed into order. Thus, for instance, unless there were storms in the atmosphere, to dissipate whatever is heterogeneous, the air could never become serene, but would become deadly by pestiferous accumulations. So in like manner in the human body, unless all things in the blood, both heterogeneous and homogeneous, did continuously and successively flow together into one heart, to be there commingled, there would be deadly conglutinations of the liquids, and they could in no way be distinctly disposed to their respective uses. (Swedenborg, Emanuel, *Arcana Coelestia* (1749-56), #842, translated by John F. Potts, 1905)

Swedenborg also understood the concept of fractals long before any contemporary mathematician because he was permitted to perceive the form of Heaven in conceptual space:

Every whole exists from various parts, since a whole without constituents is not anything; it has no form, and therefore no quality. But when a whole exists from various parts, and the various parts are in a perfect form, in which each attaches itself like a congenial friend to another in series, then the quality is perfect. So heaven is a whole from various parts arranged in a most perfect form, for the heavenly form is the most perfect of all forms. That this is the ground of all perfection is evident from the nature of all beauty, agreeableness and delight, by which the senses and the mind are affected; for these qualities spring and flow from no other source than the concert and harmony of many concordant and congenial parts, either coexisting in order or following in order, and never from a whole without many parts. From this is the saying that variety gives delight; and the nature of variety, as is known, is what determines the delight. From all this it can be seen as in a mirror how perfection comes from variety even in heaven. (Swedenborg, Emanuel, *Heaven and Hell*, 1758, Translated by John C. Ager, #56)

But the societies of which the whole heaven consists, are very numerous, and are more or less universal. The more universal are those to which an entire member, organ, or viscus, corresponds; and the less universal are those to which their parts, or parts of parts, correspond. Every society is an image of the whole, for that which is unanimous is composed of so many images of itself. As the more universal societies are images of the Grand Man, they have within them particular societies which correspond in a similar manner. (Swedenborg, Emanuel, *Arcana Coelestia* (1749-56), #4625, translated by John F. Potts, 1905)

Swedenborg eventually also discovered that the Bible is not really about such mundane things as Jacob's pottage. Like there is an underlying Reality behind the natural universe, there is a hidden Truth behind the strange and bizarre stories of the Bible. We will discover what this

Truth is in the latter part of this book. Mathematical Truth, natural Truth, conceptual Truth and Spiritual Truth are all related:

> *And Jacob boiled pottage. That this signifies a chaotic mass of doctrinal things, is evident from the representation of Jacob, as being the doctrine of natural truth, thus the doctrinal things which are in the natural man; and from the signification of "pottage," as being a chaotic mass of such things. "Boiling it," signifies amassing, for in the original tongue the expression is proper to pottage, as if it had been said that he "pottaged pottage," that is, he amassed it. The first state of the conjunction of good and truth is that which is described in this and the following verses, down to the end of the chapter.*
>
> *The first state of the man who is being regenerated, or in whom truth is being conjoined with good, is that first of all in his natural man, or in its storehouse called the memory, there are amassed the doctrinal things of truth without any certain order. The doctrinal things at that time therein may be compared to some undigested and uncompounded mass, and to a kind of chaos. But this is to the end that they may be reduced to order, for whatever is to be reduced to order is at first in this state of confusion; and this is what is signified by the pottage which Jacob boiled, that is, amassed. These doctrinal things are not reduced to order by themselves, but by the good which flows into them, and the good reduces them into order in exact proportion to the amount and the quali-*

ty of its action upon them. (Swedenborg, Emanuel, *Arcana Coelestia* (1749-56), #3316, translated by John F. Potts, 1905)

Fig. 1.22. Jacob and Esau
and the Mess of Pottage (Jan Victors, 1652)

More than 200 years ago, Swedenborg already understood that what appears simple is in reality complex. And the more simple it is, the more complex it must be. For example, a human being appears whole, discrete and simple. However, such a seemingly simple being consists of a complex network of organic cells. Each of these cells is a complex structure of DNA molecules. These molecules consist of atoms which appear to be simpler than molecules but in fact are more complex structures of elementary particles. Elementary particles appear simpler than atoms but physicists have discovered that they consist of virtual particles which in fact are more complex conceptual and emotional structures of energy (quaternions, octonions, sedenions, hypernumbers, etc).

Hence, Swedenborg concluded that if God's energy were the simplest of all, it should equally be the most complex substance of all. This is corroborated by what we discovered in the conceptual space of mathematics. We have seen that what is angular originates from the circle. The circle originates from spirals ($e^{i\pi}$). Involving and evolving spirals emerge from higher-dimensional vortices. These harmonic vortices proceed from God's Harmonic Mind or Truth and God's Harmonic Will or Love. And, if God's energy is infinitely coherent or the simplest of all substances, it must also be infinitely complex. In God, infinite simplicity and infinite complexity are harmonized. However, in the universe, God is present as the Law of Truth and the Freedom of Love.

Chapter 2

NATURAL BEAUTY:

LIFE

In the last chapter, we conjectured that the universe is probably a fractal that is being generated from conceptual space by the harmonic fractal generator of Divine Love. Divine Love or God's Transcendental Energy is infinitely complex and harmonically organized. This organization is Divine Wisdom or Truth. If this is true, we should not only detect order and disorder in the universe; we should equally find evidence of order emerging from chaos. Furthermore, the constants e, i, π and φ should manifest in the laws and structures of the universe. According to Chaos theory, when disorder reaches its critical maximum point, harmony is reestablished by an attractor. In this chapter, we are going to explore the physical universe and determine if there is evidence to substantiate this claim.

Scientists tell us that the physical universe is being generated from the quantum field. But, although quantum theory has been verified countless times by experiment, it continues to be a source of problems for scientists. This is because the wave-function of quantum mechanics is only able to generate probabilities of actual events. According to quantum theory, quanta are emerging randomly from the quantum foam. And it is the act of observation which collapses the wave-function and causes an actual event to occur. Our approach is different. We are saying that the physical universe is being generated from conceptual space by means of the harmonic fractal generator of Divine Love. This fractal generator is an infinite complexity that is organized harmonically. This is why we may detect randomness or chaotic behavior in the universe as well as order. But Chaos and Order are always linked by a strange attractor. The parts of the universe may be free to act, react and interact but their actions, reactions and interactions are governed by the whole.

Therefore, we are assuming or postulating that conceptual space is as real as physical space. And the universe is perpetually being generated from the omnipresence of conceptual space by Divine Love. Conceptual space and physical space must not only be discrete and separate; they must also be in *correspondence*. Every object in physical space must be in correspondence with a concept in conceptual space. This is because the universe is the physical manifestation of God's process. This would mean that the Divine Energy Field of Love must be in correspondence with some energy field in physical space. What is this field?

Love not only involves and evolves harmonically in conceptual space; it also attracts all concepts into its infinite harmonic vortex. The strange attractor of Love is emotional magnetism. This would explain where physical magnetism originates. Love or emotional magnetism must be in *correspondence* with physical magnetism. Just as Love connects and relates all ideas and emotions in conceptual space, physical magnetism must connect all things in physical space. Like our brain and our mind, physical magnetism and emotional magnetism (Love) must be in two radically discrete and different spaces. Physical magnetism is in physical space and Love is in conceptual space. But they are linked by *correspondence* (Fig. 2.1).

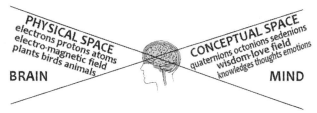

Fig.2.1. Correspondence between
Physical and Conceptual Space

The harmonic and perpetual involution and evolution of Divine Love (Fig. 2.2) must cause the magnetic field to twist and generate electrical charge and discharge. This is where the polarities of positive and negative electricity must originate. In $e^{i\pi}$, e is the growth of the magnetic field, i is time or curvature and π is the rate at which it grows. This fractal expansion-contraction or explosion-implosion is also eventually responsible for universal gravitation and the generation of matter and physical space. When the magnetic field is twisted by the gyroscope of Love, the electromagnetic field of Light is generated. This is how God created and continues to generate the physical universe. God is continually generating photons or quanta from conceptual space. If this is true, then these quanta of Light must always be in correspondence with Love and Truth. Truth must be conceptual light and Love must be emotional heat (energy). God must be generating the universe from His Love and Truth.

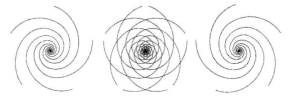

Fig. 2.2. Involution – Realization - Evolution

Here, we discover that there is nothing uncertain about the quantum field or the wave-function of quantum mechanics. The wave-function is a wave-function of possibilities. It tells us what is possible in the universe. What is possible is in correspondence with Divine Love or God's will. According to quantum physicists, the absolute product of the wave-function and its complex conjugate results in a probability of 1 or certainty. They postulate that it is the act of observation or measurement which collapses the wave-function and causes a possibility to become actual. However, Willie Johnson Jr. has discovered that the wave-function can also be described as a *space centrode*[1], its conjugate is a *body centrode*, and the product of the wavefunction and its complex conjugate is equal to the relationship and interaction of quaternions:

$$- \Psi \Psi* = -1 = e^{i\pi} = ijk = i^2 = j^2 = k^2$$

$$|\Psi \Psi*| = 1$$

The product of all the constants of nature are equal to $|\Psi\Psi*|$ or unity. What does all this mean? Essentially, this means that, although all the parts of the universe can freely act and interact with each other, only those parts that are in HARMONY are able to collapse the wave-function and evolve or return to Love. If this is true, then the laws of the physical universe should reflect this truth. And, in fact, we do discover that all the laws of the physical universe are essentially laws of CONSERVATION, EQUILIBRIUM, SYMMETRY and HARMONY. And most of them can be derived from the principle of *stationary action*. Stationary action must be how God or the Infinite One acts in the physical universe. Divine Love is God's will. Divine Truth is God's plan or Divine Idea. This Divine Idea includes all the harmonic possibilities embedded in the wave-function of the universe. And God is realizing His plan by means of *stationary action*.

---

1   A space centrode is the path traced by the instantaneous center of a rotating body moving relative to an inertial frame of reference. See Johnson Jr., Willie, *The Sagitta Key*, Lulu Books, August 30, 2014.

Incidentally or providentially, it was also William Rowan Hamilton, the discoverer of quaternions, who formulated the *principle of stationary action*. Given a dynamic system, conventionally, such a system is expressed by differential equations which describe how position and momentum change with time. However, by the principle of stationary action, such a system can be expressed by using an integral and minimizing the value of the integral. Action is a product of energy and time. And the action of the system integrated over an interval of time is always minimal. In fact, most of the laws of the universe can be derived using this approach.

When we think about it, *stationary action* is paradoxical. How can something act and yet be stationary? But this is exactly how God acts in the universe. He remains constant or stationary but He continually acts. Divine Love acts like a gyroscope. An integral in calculus is an anti-derivative. By taking the integral, we are determining how all the parts are acting as a whole. And, by minimizing the integral, we are assuming that the system is in equilibrium or in harmony with the whole. What the principle of stationary action tells us is that, although all parts in the universe are free to act and interact, these actions and interactions are regulated by the whole or the gyroscope of Love. And if the whole is synonymous with God, then it means that it is God that is in control of the whole universe. God is omnipresent, omniscient and omnipotent through the gyroscope of Love.

In order to derive the laws of the physical universe by means of stationary action, physicists use integrals and assume that the system will essentially be governed by the whole. Due to the principle of stationary action, the universe is in a state of dynamic equilibrium. Each part is free to act and interact. However, since each part is connected to all other parts as well as to the whole, every interaction affects the whole universe. This equally means that the whole is in every part.

Although most scientists still insist that the wave-function collapses through observation, David Bohm had a causal interpretation of quantum theory. He postulated that the universe was governed by a *holomovement* or movement of the whole. And this holomovement of unfoldment and enfoldment was embedded within every part of the universe. Hence, the collapse of the wave-function would be caused by the generative order or holomovement itself. In fact, he used the analogy of the hologram to explain his theory of implicate and explicate order. In a hologram, the information of the whole 3-D image is in every part of the hologram. And, even if a hologram is shattered into many parts, the information of the whole image can still be recovered within any part, although it is not as clear. This becomes even more valid when we discover that Dennis Gabor, the inventor of holography, used the Fourier transform to generate holograms. The Fourier transform of g(t) is G(f):

$$G(f) = \int_{-\infty}^{\infty} g(t)e^{-2\pi i ft}dt$$

Here, we find the principle of stationary action and our harmonic fractal generator expressed in this equation. Every 3-D manifestation is a wave-function of standing waves and this wave-function contains an image of the whole universe within itself. Thus, all parts of the universe are self-similar images of the whole universe. According to what we have discovered, these would be self-similar images of Divine love.

Since the universe is generated from the freedom of Love, there is a certain degree of freedom on every level of the universe and order may degenerate into disorder. However, when this disorder reaches its maximum point, the attractor of Divine Love causes order to again emerge from chaos. This is because the universe is feeding back upon itself. Every thing proceeds from Divine Love and returns to Divine Love. To our physical eyes, this kind of self-organization seems almost unnatural or miraculous. But this is because the attractor of Love is in conceptual space, not physical space.

Now, in order to understand how the physical universe is generated from conceptual space, we must erase all our preconceived ideas about physical space, matter and time. For example, the universe of space and matter is in reality a field of energy that is being formed from conceptual space. Every physical object consists of energy; this is its substance. Its wavefunction of standing waves represents its structure or form. And its action or process can be derived from the principle of stationary action. This principle also describes the laws by which its action is governed. This equally means that time is non-linear. Events are not only constrained by the history of the past; they are also influenced by the possibilities of the future state of the universe. And this future state can only be a state of Universal Love where the Infinite One or God is harmonically conjoined with all created beings.

Beyond the magnetic field, there is nothing physical. The so-called virtual particles of the quantum field are not in physical space; they are in conceptual space. These are the spinors, twistors or quaternions, octonions, sedenions and hypernumbers that are driving or propelling the whole physical universe from Divine Love. Beyond the quantum, there is no mass, no physical space, no charge and no time. The quantum is a quantum of action. And this stationary action is Love in action.

Therefore, the physical universe begins in the electromagnetic field. Divine Love causes the magnetic field to twist and generate the physical universe. The positive and negative polarities of electricity result from the twisting or involution and evolution of the magnetic field. This is why most elementary particles are conjugates. Quarks, electrons, positrons, protons and neutrons are all conjugates. Maxwell's laws of electromagnetism describe how magnetism and electricity interact. And the electric field and magnetic field are at right angles to each other because they are conjugates. In fact, Maxwell originally utilized quaternions to describe the laws of electromagnetism by means of twenty equations. These equations were truncated by Oliver Heaviside into four vector equations. In Heaviside's equations, the process of enfoldment into conceptual space is completely absent. This is why scientists continue to have such a materialistic view of the universe. They are ignoring the fact that all things are also enfolding or re-turning into conceptual space.

Fig. 2.3. Tracks Made from Subtomic Particles

According to W. Johnson Jr., matter and space are conjugates. The whole universe precesses. Inertia and gravity are conjugates. This is why galaxies are expanding toward the outer peripheries of the universe according to Hubble's law. Most celestial objects are also essentially gyroscopes that rotate and revolve around gravitational centers and precess. Involution is a centrifugal force which causes the expansion of the universe. And Newton's law of universal gravitation can be derived from the principle of stationary action.

In figure 2.3, we can also see how subatomic particles are behaving; they are spiraling in and out of existence. Most elementary particles also spin, rotate, revolve and precess because they are in correspondence with the spinors or quaternions of conceptual space. Physical space and matter (mass) are also conjugates. Physical space results from involution and matter is spawned through evolution. Johnson discovered that space and matter can be represented by two cones (space and body centrodes) that are tangent to each other and spinning in opposite directions. Remember mass is equivalent to energy. Centers of mass are produced when waves of energy interact HARMONICALLY or coherently and fractally collapse (implode) into the vortex of Love. An atom consists of standing waves of energy sustained by harmonic Love.

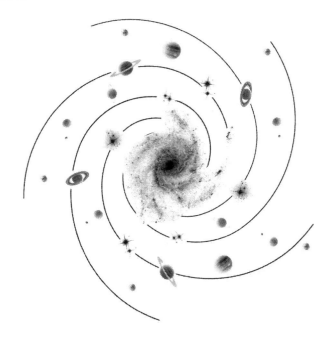

Fig. 2.4. The Involution of the Universe

Matter is caused by evolution or a return to Love. This is the force and law of gravitation. Now, when we combine these two harmonic conjugates of expansion and gravitation, we should obtain something harmonious and beautiful. And, in fact, this results in *the music of the spheres* or the celestial and harmonic dance of galaxies, stars and planets in physical space. The center of each galaxy is a black hole that is in correspondence with conceptual space and the vortical generator of Divine Love (Fig. 2.4).

After billions and billions of years of iteration, the universe becomes filled with billions of galaxies. And each of these galaxies consists of millions of stars such as our own sun. Most of these stars involve and evolve as stellar systems which incorporate gaseous and mineral planets, earths and moons such as those found in our own solar system. And all bodies in the atomic world as well as in the celestial world are self-similar images of Divine Love.

Fig. 2.5. Galaxies, Stars , Planets and Moons

There is ample evidence in the firmament to substantiate that galaxies, stars and planets were formed and continue to evolve in correspondence with the fractal generator of Divine Love. The shape of younger galaxies is spiral, and most older ones are elliptical. Stars, planets and moons are spherical. Moreover, celestial objects spin upon their axis, revolve around gravitational centers and precess like gyroscopes (Fig. 2.5) The whole universe is spinning, revolving and precessing because it is re-turning to Love.

Is there evidence in the physical heavens that the universe is a fractal? Well, in order to determine the validity of this conclusion we would need to determine how galaxies are arranged or ordered in the physical heavens. Astronomers have determined that galaxies are bundled into galaxy clusters of thousands of galaxies held together by gravity. But how are these bundles of galaxies ordered? Modern day instruments are still unable to detect such large scales. However, recently, some astronomers have been able to produce computer simulations of such an organization. In figure 2.6. we can see such a simulation or model on the left. And this organization is strangely similar to the organization of the neural networks of the human brain (on the right).

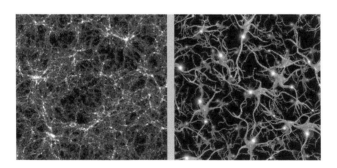

Fig. 2.6. Left-Network of Galaxy Clusters
Right- Network of Human Neurons

This discovery is in agreement with our prior discussions. But what does it imply? It suggests that the universe is not the outcome of chance or accident. Galaxies are not randomly scattered in space; they are ordered in a complex and chaotic system like the neurons of the human brain. In fact, we can even speculate that the whole universe may be organized like a human fractal. And this would also explain why the ultimate result of natural evolution of biological life on earth culminated in the human form. The whole universe must be evolving toward this form. And, if Divine Love is the universe's fractal generator, this also means that Divine Love must resemble the complexity of the human form. The complex organization and interaction of hypernumbers, sedenions, octonions and quaternions must be similar to the complexity of the human form. The only difference is that these spinors and twistors are describing the harmonic and complex organization of Divine Truth in conceptual space. The human form must be the physical representation of Divine Truth, which is the form of Divine Love. Incidentally, this was also confirmed by Swedenborg when he was conscious in the fields of Heaven.

This discovery will undoubtedly help us understand the intricacies of natural evolution. Scientists tell us that it all began with Hydrogen, the most abundant atomic element in the physical universe. The material universe evolved from clouds of Hydrogen atoms. Stars are born through nuclear fusion. When lighter nuclei such as those of Hydrogen fuse into Helium, they release energy in the form of Light. However, this is all occurring in correspondence with the fractal generator of Divine Love:

And God said, "Let there be light," and there was light. Genesis 1:3

The beginning of the world was the spoken thought of God. This is the "Let there be light! " at which a visible and beautiful world springs into being out of chaos and darkness. While things are in darkness, it is as if they were not. It is as the light appears that they take shape, and have a definite, cognizable existence. The mass of clay before the artist is as chaos; the idea broods over it, and breathes itself into it, like the Spirit of the Creator over the face of the deep. The Word, the forming idea, goes from the artist into the clay, moulding that into form which had no form, and making each part to be a related part, or part of a whole; thus distinguished from, at the same time that it is united to, other parts. (Sewall, Frank, *The New Metaphysics*, 1888)

A star, like our own sun, is essentially a solar dynamo. And a dynamo is an electrical generator that produces electricity and magnetism from kinetic energy or the energy of motion. This energy is produced from the convection of plasma as the sun converts Hydrogen ions into Helium atoms by atomic fusion. Thus, we can speculate that the periodic table of natural elements was vortically generated during billions of years of natural evolution. In fact, the atomic elements can be arranged vortically (Fig.2.7). Atoms of increasing density are produced when waves of energy interact coherently and collapse or return into the harmonic vortex of Divine Love. This is how the nucleus of every atom is formed. Every atom consists of standing waves of energy and its nucleus is always in correspondence with the stable gyroscope of Divine Love.

The periodic table of atomic elements also consists of harmonic conjugates in the atomic world. Except for the noble gases, which are electronically stable, most atomic elements are seeking conjugates. Elements that are complementary are able to react and combine to form more stable harmonic compounds or molecules. They do this by the sharing of electrons. For example, when Sodium (Na) and Chlorine (Cl) interact, they form the more stable compound of NaCl, Sodium Chloride or salt. Two Hydrogen atoms and one Oxygen atom integrate to produce the stable molecule of H_2O or water. This would mean that only those atoms that are in harmony are able to form bonds and produce molecules that are stable. A molecule is a stable organization of standing waves of energy.

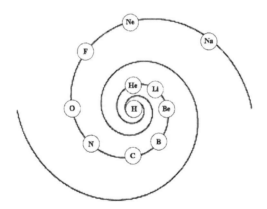

Fig. 2.7. Vortical Periodic Table of Atomic Elements

Although solids, liquids and gases on earth appear to be formless, their atomic structure tends to display symmetry and harmony. The Platonic solids are the five essential ways points can be harmonically connected by lines in 3-d space. This may be why this symmetry is equally displayed in the formation of atomic bonds as well as the generation of crystals. The Vertices, Edges and Faces in each Platonic solid are related according to Euler's formula for polyhedra:

$$V - E + F = 2$$

It is also an interesting fact that only the tetrahedron, cube and octahedron can be detected in the formation of natural crystals. The icosahedron and dodecahedron tend to be found in molecules of organic life. This is also probably why the Golden Ratio, φ, can be found in the inner proportions of these two Platonic solids.

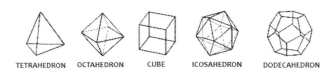

TETRAHEDRON   OCTAHEDRON   CUBE   ICOSAHEDRON   DODECAHEDRON

Fig. 2.8. Platonic Solids

On earth, the gases of the atmosphere, the waters of oceans, seas and lakes, and the natural formations of the mineral world seem to have no specific forms. However, it is equally true that the earthly landscape of mountains, hills, lakes, islands, beaches and coastlines erodes, transforms and evolves fractally with time. And the history of ancient civilizations and extinct species such as as dinosaurs becomes embedded in the strata of the earth's crust. Moreover, we can readily detect the strange attractor of Love in the fractal organization of clouds, the rhythm of waves in the vastness of the ocean, whirlpools in rivers, and most vividly in the shape of hurricanes and tornadoes. In figure 2.9, we can see how hurricane Katrina was formed in the natural atmosphere. Hurricanes are the most powerful evidence that processes are behaving according to Chaos Theory.

Fig. 2.9. Hurricane Katrina

Besides the climate and weather, there is more proof that the landscape of the earth is involving, evolving and transforming fractally. This can be seen in the evolving shapes of coastlines, islands, beaches, rocks and mountains. In figure 2.10, we can see part of the coastline of Norway. Geographically, Norway is characterized by large fjords and thousands of islands. The fjords are deep grooves in the land produced by floods from the sea after the Ice Age. The coastline of Norway was generated over a long period of time by glacial erosion. We can see that this coastline has evolved through many iterations like a fractal. The fjords have diverged fractally over time like the branches of a tree.

Fig. 2.10. Fractal Coastline of Norway

We do not need to remain on the coast; we can equally move inland and discover more fractal structures. The Alps form an extensive mountain range (750 miles) in Europe. They stretch across Austria, France, Germany, Italy, Liechtenstein, Monaco, Slovenia, and Switzerland. These high mountains were formed over millions of years from the dynamic interaction between tectonic plates within the earth's crust. During these events, sedimentary rocks were compelled to thrust upward and generate mountains. Once again, this was a gradual unfolding and enfolding over very long periods of time. In figure 2.11, we can see an overhead view of the Alps. And this fractal structure is also very similar to the branch structure of a tree or the vessels and nerves of the human organism.

Fig. 2.11. Fractal Structure of the Alps

The many chemical compounds that evolved over the ages on planet Earth were essentially generated and formed from the fractal harmonic generator of Love by correspondence and influx. The perpetual vortical e-motion or involution and evolution of Love sustains, maintains and restores all physical processes. Thus, only those atoms that were able to combine harmonically reached stability. And all other combinations were naturally disintegrated. Thus, we can conclude that the complex molecules of nucleic acids, proteins and carbohydrates that ultimately evolved on planet Earth were generated, sustained and maintained by the fractal generator of

Love. This is essentially why the DNA molecule is a double helix.

When we study the DNA molecule, there is ample evidence to suggest that this miraculous structure was designed and built up through involution and evolution from conceptual fields of higher intelligence. For example, the atoms are arranged vortically according to the Golden Ratio, φ. The power of DNA resides in its ability to duplicate (Fig. 2.12). DNA is able to split and form an exact copy of itself. When we further explore the structure of DNA, we can see how the two helices of molecules are a physical manifestation of the harmonic conjugate spirals of involution and evolution in conceptual space.

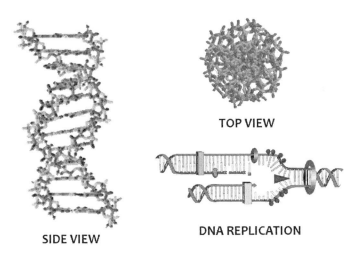

TOP VIEW

DNA REPLICATION

SIDE VIEW

Fig. 2.12. Organization and Replication of DNA

DNA is found in the fundamental unit of biological life: the living organic cell. Living organic beings consist of billions of organic cells structured according to the form of the species. When we observe how cells multiply and arrange themselves fractally in the form of the organism, it seems almost like a miraculous process. However, when we realize that such organisms are essentially standing waves of energy that are generated, propelled, sustained and restored by the fractal generator and attractor of Divine Love, such processes become understandable.

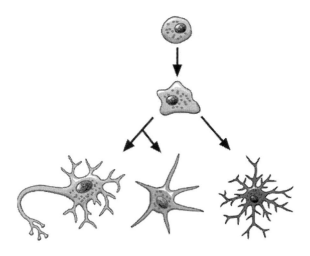

Fig. 2.13. Types of Organic Cells

Every organic cell consists of cytoplasm enclosed within a membrane, which contains proteins and nucleic acids. The DNA and RNA molecules, which embed the information, heredity and intelligence of the species form the nucleus of the cell. Stem cells differentiate and evolve into specialized cells that eventually carry out the necessary work in the different parts of the body (Fig. 2.13). For example, nerve cells or neurons, which resemble trees, form the nervous system and the brain. The nucleus of every cell in a living organism is in fact a complex vortex that enfolds the whole history of biological life on earth. Such a vortex is also connected by correspondence to the fractal attractor of Love.

The kingdom of flora or plant life is a rich, endlessly diverse, elegant and beautiful display of colors and forms in our physical world. And there is more than enough evidence to suggest that these species are all evolving and growing fractally. In fact, it is in the plant world where we find the most elegant fractals. These fractals are understandably less complex than animal or human structures because plants evolved from minerals, animals evolved from plants and humans evolved from animals. And, although this evolution was a continuous process, these kingdoms of organic life are discrete and separate.

Fig. 2.14. The Unfolding Growth of a Rose

When we contemplate the blooming of flowers, we can understand why Swedenborg discovered that flowers represent memory-knowledges of Truth in the spiritual world. The rose in figure 2.14 is unfolding from a bud. And the organization of its petals is almost identical to the attractor of Love. This may also be why the sight and scent of flowers tend to evoke feelings of pure Love in most human beings. The fragrance of most flowers is as harmonious and pleasant as the gracefulness of their form. When we observe the shape of a flower, we are seeing Truth physically manifested. But flowers are in physical space while Truth is in conceptual space.

Fig. 2.15. Bleeding Heart Flower

The whole of nature is a book where we can perceive meaning and purpose. This is because every object in physical space is in correspondence with a concept in conceptual space. Swedenborg discovered that ancient civilizations were able to understand the universe and communicate with the heavens of conceptual space by using the *science of correspondences.* This Heavenly science explained how all things in the natural world corresponded to spiritual or conceptual realities. In fact, astrology is a vestige of this ancient science. However, when humanity fell spiritually, this science was lost and veiled. Eventually, the human race was provided with the Bible by which to understand God's Word or Truth. And every word in the Bible corresponds to a spiritual reality because the Bible was also written by means of the *science of correspondences*. The bleeding heart flower of figure 2.15 is perhaps a picture of what happened after the fall of man. Man disconnected from Heaven and God, and he began to worship the world and his own self. When we lose the Love of God, we equally lose His Truth.

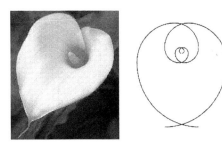

Fig. 2.16. The Arium Flower

Most flowers consist of many petals but we should perhaps begin with the simplest flower. The arium is an elegant flower that seems to unfold as a single petal. However, when we look at figure 2.16 , we can see that it is the result of involving and evolving spirals. The growth of all natural fractals is propelled by these spirals of involution and evolution. The nucleus of a flower is usually where its reproductive organs are located because this inner core is always in connection with the fractal generator of Love.

Pine trees are born from fertilized pine seeds. But these seeds are encased within a pine cone. Female cones contain ovules while male cones contain pollen. When the ovules are fertilized by pollen, they become seeds. And, when the cone matures, the seeds are able to dislodge from between the plates of the cone. It is difficult to detect any geometry in tiny pine seeds but pine cones display geometrical forms that are not too difficult to recognize (Fig. 2.17).

Fig. 2.17. Pine Cone and Golden Ratio

Many plants consist mainly of large leaves. And leaves also contain veins that are unmistakably fractal. For example, when we admire a fern in nature, we are entranced by the harmonic and fractal order of its leaves. Every leaf on every scale is an image of the whole fern. But we would become even more astounded if we realized that such a fern can be generated by a mathematical equation. In figure 2.18, we can see the photo image of a natural fern. And beside it is a graphical fern generated from a mathematical algorithm on a computer. Now, when we compare the two images, we notice that the mathemati-

cal fern is ideal and almost perfect. But this is perhaps because it did not have to adapt to the uncertainties and
harshness of its environment during its evolution and
growth like the real fractal.

Fig.2.18. Natural and Mathematical Fern

The whole vegetable kingdom is a physical manifestation of mathematical harmony in nature. At first glance,
when we look at a vegetable like okra for example, we
would not suspect that it embeds any geometrical properties that we can recognize. However, when we dig somewhat deeper, we can see that its inner and outer structure
evolved with mathematical precision. The cross-section of
okra in figure 2.19 reveals that its seeds are arranged and
encased in a pentagonal structure. And we have seen that
the number 5 is characteristic of biological life. The Gold-
en Ratio can also be expressed as an equation which includes the number 5:

$$\varphi = (1 + \sqrt{5}) / 2$$

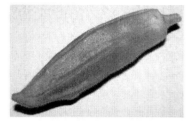 

Fig. 2.19. The Geometrical Structure of Okra

Many other vegetables, such as broccoli and cabbage, also grow fractally and mathematically in rhythm with the fractal generator of Divine Love. The fractal generated as Romanesco broccoli is particularly striking (Fig. 2.20). Every cone on all levels of this broccoli fractal is similar to the whole cone. When we cut through most vegetables and fruits, we can almost see a picture of how they have involved and evolved over time. As living species evolve, this chaotic fractal becomes increasingly complex but it retains its coherence. For example, it seems almost miraculous that an organism as complex as the human body can grow from a tiny fertilized ovum. But we know that this organized complexity has taken billions of years to evolve.

The seashells that we often find scattered on most beaches are the protective layers of invertebrate animals, molluscs, barnacles, horseshoe crabs and brachiopods. When a mollusc dies and its soft inner parts have been eaten by other fish in the sea, its hard outer shell remains and eventually washes up on the beach. Most of these seashells are beautiful representations of involving and evolving fractals. And many people use them as decorative items in their home as well as ornamental jewelry. However, we are more interested in their mathematical structure. We can readily conclude from the inner and outer structure of its shell that a mollusc, such as a nautilus, grows fractally. And its outer shell is a three-dimensional representation of the Golden Ratio in nature (Fig. 2.21).

Fig. 2.20. Romanesco Broccoli and Cabbage

As we have seen, the Golden Ratio can be readily detected in plant species as well as primitive animals such as molluscs. However, as biological species become more complex and intricate, this harmonic proportion becomes increasingly difficult to identify. This is because the fractal generator of Love is in reality infinitely complex and harmonic. And, as living species become more compounded and convoluted, the real harmonic structure and intelligence of Love is being displayed. For example, birds are very different from plants, molluscs or fish because they have adapted to the wind and the air by evolving wings.

However, the Golden Ratio is still hidden within their inner and outer structure (Fig. 2.22).

Fig. 2.21. Golden Ratio in Sea shells

Birds are able to fly in the air by flapping their wings. This is a remarkable evolutionary achievement when we think about it. But all evolution is a desire of Love to express or manifest itself as Life. Fish needed to adapt to the watery environment of the ocean. As a result, Love generated their fins to swim and their tail as a rudder. Wings are much wider and more muscular because it is more difficult to stand or balance in the air than in the sea. In order to stay up in the air, birds must produce a standing wave by flapping their wings up and down perpetually (Fig. 2.23). And we have also seen that all created beings are in fact standing waves in an ocean of Love. As humans, we are linked to Love by the beating of our heart, the inhaling and exhaling of our breath and the cycle of our sleep and wakefulness.

Fig. 2.22. Golden Ratio in Parrot Form

Fig. 2.23. Flying Bird and Standing Wave

Many of us are impressed by the workings of nature. We wonder how plants know exactly how to grow as of themselves. And many behaviors and actions in the animal kingdom are equally amazing. How do bees know how to form hives with mathematical precision? How does a spider know how to weave its spiraling web? From birth, every animal knows exactly which food is appropriate for its body and which foods to avoid. Every species of animals also has intricate and complex mating rituals that allow it to procreate. For example, salmon are born in fresh water but live in the ocean. And, in order to procreate, they instinctively migrate and return to fresh water lakes to mate. The migration of birds is equally wondrous. However, when we realize that God's Wisdom inflows by correspondence into every being in the universe and informs it on how to realize its purpose, these amazing behaviors become understandable. God is omnipresent with every being in the universe through His Love and He understands and instructs every being though His omniscient Wisdom.

We have seen that biological species are not only impelled and guided by the intelligent attractor of Love; they must equally adapt to their particular and uncertain environment. Their fractal structure is continually unfolding in physical space and enfolding into conceptual space. By living in its outer environment, a biological creature is learning to adapt. And this intelligence is enfolded within its memory as waves of energy within its being. This intelligence is also present in its reproductive seeds and is eventually past on to future generations by heredity.

Through involution and evolution, the fractal generator of Love is producing images of itself. And we have seen that these images are becoming more complex, freer and more intelligent. Most of these species have taken millions of years to evolve. Mathematically, we could say that their fractal structure was generated by means of billions and billions of iterations. With every subsequent iteration, the fractal of the universe becomes more complex, freer and more intelligent. And, since the attractor of this fractal is Divine Love, the species that are generated resemble Divine Love more and more.

Fig. 2.24. Involving and Evolving Spirals of Love
Manifested in Ram Horns

Most reptiles and birds do not have very graceful faces. In fact, for the most part, their faces seem menacing and cruel. However, land mammals, such as rams, deer and sheep have gentler expressions that tend to resemble the human face. When we reach the world of mammals, complexity has also increased to such an extent that we have difficulty detecting the characteristic spirals of involution and evolution. Most land mammals have four feet and no hands to defend themselves. However, many species do have horns growing from their foreheads. In fact, this is how Love expresses its power in the animal world. Most of these gentle animals use their horns as a defense mechanism. In the Israelitish Church, these horns were employed as trumpets because they expressed the power of Truth (Word of God). And it is plainly apparent that ram's horns manifest the involution and evolution spirals of Love on the physical level (Fig. 2.24).

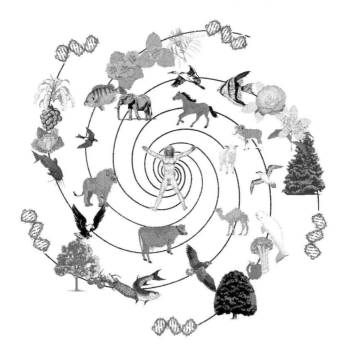

Fig. 2.25. Evolution of Matter into Organic Complexity

Following a few hundred million more years of iteration, the human species was ultimately generated. Now, we know that man enfolds all the evolution of biological life on earth. And, although he embeds the intelligence and memories of plant, fish, bird and animal species within his being, he subsists in a different, discrete and separate kingdom. From studying the DNA structure of apes such as chimpanzees (90% similar) and comparing it to the human genome, many scientists have erroneously been led to conclude that humans are simply more complex intelligent apes. However, it is also a fact that the human genome has much in common with other living species such as yeast (18%), banana (50%), fish (70%), cow (80%), and cat (90%).

A human being may have a high percentage of DNA in common with apes, but a human being is definitely not an ape. Humans subsist in a completely discrete category. How are humans different from animals? When we investigate the world of animals, we may notice that some apes are able to stand upright and use their hands to produce and use tools. Penguins can stand upright and some parrots can also mimic the sounds of human speech. However, from careful observation, we are led to conclude that animals do not have the power of the Word or speech. And this is because words are in correspondence with ideas of the mind. Animals do not have access to spiritual or conceptual ideas because they are natural beings that only possess a natural mind. Unlike animals, humans are complete images of God because their (free)will is an image of Love, their mind is an image of Truth and their Action is an image of Divine Power. They are free to love, free to think and free to do. Humans are able to reconcile natural energy and spiritual energy. They may exist in physical space but they equally subsist in conceptual space. Humanity is the complete reflected image of Divine

Love. And this is confirmed in the Bible where we learn that God generated man in His own image and likeness.

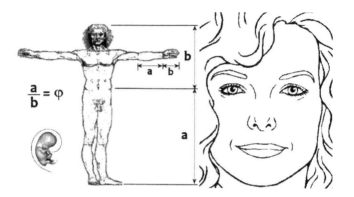

Fig. 2.26. Golden Ratio in Human Body and Face

We can see in figure 2.25 that human beings are the culmination of natural evolution. Through natural evolution, the fractal generator of Love has produced a full image of itself. In fact, the human form must be the physical representation of the infinitely complex and harmonized fractal generator of Love. It is a physical image of the relationship between spinors, twistors, quaternions, octonions, sedenions and beyond in conceptual space. When we admire the delicate, warm and graceful face of a human being, we are in fact seeing the form of Love manifested in the flesh. Now, we know that man was generated as male and female from the start. And, in effect, male and female, like all things in the universe, are harmonic conjugates. This is because everything was generated through the harmonic conjugates of Love and Wisdom. In

God, Love and Wisdom are infinitely harmonized. However, in lower dimensions, Love manifests as the chirality of right and left. The fractal generator of Love manifests as the left-handed spiral of involution and the right-handed spiral of evolution. In our 3-d world, our left hand is the mirror image of our right hand. But these two spins or conjugates are harmonized in a higher dimension.

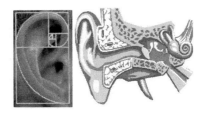

Fig. 2.27. Golden Spiral in Outer and Inner Ear

Now, when we studied quaternions, we discovered that they were related in a vortex. Hence, we can speculate that the human form must be a very complex vortex. And every vortex has a nucleus, center or vortical attractor. This is especially evident in hurricanes. The center, nucleus or attractor is where waves interfere, collapse and return. In the human organism, we should also find such an attractor. The human structure must be a vortex where waves of energy interfere, collapse and return to conceptual space.

When we study human anatomy and keep in mind what we now know, we are able to understand the mysteries of the human body. First, there is certainly enough evidence to conclude that the human form is structured

according to the Golden Ratio. For example, the height of
the whole human body to the height of the navel, the
length of the whole human face to the height of the eyes,
the length of the forearm to the length of the hand are all
equal to φ (Fig. 2.26). And there are countless other ex-
amples. For instance, in order to analyze sound waves,
the outer and inner ear is completely organized in accordance with a Golden spiral (Fig. 2.27).

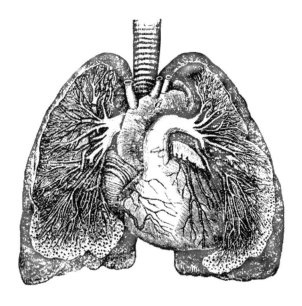

Fig. 2.28. Attractor of Heart and Lungs

As we have already noted, the symmetry of the human
structure is the result of chirality. Every human organ,
member or gland tends to consist of harmonic conju-

gates. For example, the right and left cerebrum hemi-spheres, eyes, ears, nostrils, lungs, arms, legs, hands, feet, kidneys, ovaries and gonads are all harmonic conjugates. But these harmonic conjugates are usually reconciled vor-tically. It is also important to notice that the human struc-ture is a vortex of three levels. Essentially, these levels are the head, where the brain is located, the thorax, which en-cases the heart and lungs and the abdomen, where the stomach, liver and kidneys are found. Hence, the human body is a vortex of three levels that is digesting and trans-forming organic, mental and emotional energy.

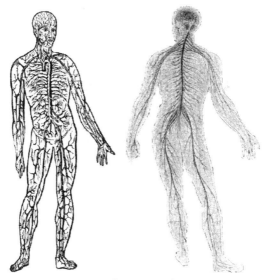

Fig. 2.29. Human Circulatory and Nervous Systems

Now, we can readily notice that the heart and lungs form an attractor where the blood is processed (Fig.

2.28), the cerebellum and cerebrum form a nucleus where electromagnetic light impressions are metabolized, and the stomach, intestines, kidneys and liver are the location where organic food is digested and processed. It can also be readily noticed that the circulatory and nervous systems have been generated as fractals that diverge and branch out throughout the whole human body (Fig. 2.29). The systolic and diastolic beating of the heart circulates oxygenated blood cells throughout the body while the brain sends and receives electromagnetic energy through neurons or nerve cells.

Like the heart and lungs, the cerebellum and cerebrum form an attractor for the nervous system. In large part, modern science has neglected the importance and significance of the cerebellum in favor of the complexity of the cerebrum. But Swedenborg has discovered that the cerebellum is quintessential because, like the heart, it corresponds to man's will. And the essence of man is his will or freedom to Love. The cerebrum, like the lungs, only represents man's understanding or beliefs. But what a human being believes is intrinsically connected to what he loves. Man's cerebellum or will is the fractal generator and attractor of his beliefs.

The human cerebral cortex is neural tissue that enfolds and unfolds in order to increase the surface area that is able to fit in the limited volume of the skull. We have already seen how this is accomplished by fractal dimensions. In fact, the human brain is the attractor of a very extensive fractal neural network. In figure 2.30, we can see the cross-section of the cerebellum. And we are able to recognize that it is very similar to the fractal coastlines that we have already encountered.

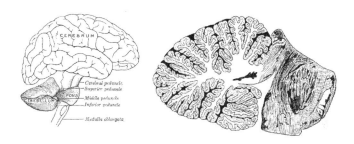

Fig. 2.30. Human Brain
and Fractal Structure of Cerebellum

It is equally interesting that the convolutions of the human cerebral cortex are called *gyri* (Fig.2.31). And we have seen that the fractal generator of the universe is a gyrator or gyroscope. The universe also unfolds and enfolds, or involves and evolves. It has involved from conceptual space until it generated the human physical form. Hence, we can conclude that the neural network of the human brain is a very complex vortex that is reflecting or reciprocating Divine Love.

In order to realize how vast, complex, chaotic and fractal the whole human organism is, we just need to take note of some actual facts. The total surface area of the human intestines is about 2700 square feet. The approximate total length of the blood vessels is 60, 000 miles and their surface area is 10,000 square feet. Finally, the entire length of the nervous system is 90,000 miles. This is almost four times the circumference of planet Earth. There is no doubt that the human physical structure is a complex chaotic fractal but this fractal must be in correspondence with an even more astounding fractal in conceptual space. Swedenborg was able to corroborate that the substances of the human brain are in correspondence with the stars of the physical Heavens and the Truths of the conceptual Heavens:

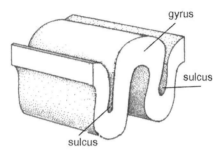

Fig. 2.31. A Gyrus of the Human Cerebral Cortex

Such as life is in its first principles, such it is in the whole and in every part. That this may be perceived, it shall now be told where in the brains these first principles are, and how they become derivative. Anatomy shows where in the brains these first principles are; it teaches that there are two brains; that these are continued from the head into the spinal column; that they consist of two substances, called cortical substance and medullary substance; that cortical substance consists of innumerable gland-like forms, and medullary substance of innumerable fiber-like forms. Now as these little glands are heads of fibrils, they are also their first principles. For from these, fibers begin and thereupon go forth, gradually bundling themselves into nerves. These bundles or nerves, when formed, descend to the organs of sense in the face, and to the organs of motion in the body, and form them. Consult any one skilled in the science of anatomy, and you will be convinced.

This cortical or glandular substance constitutes the surface of the cerebrum, and also the surface of the corpora striata, from which proceeds the medulla oblongata; it also constitutes the middle of the cerebellum, and the middle of the spinal marrow. But medullary or fibrillary substance everywhere begins in and proceeds from the cortical; out of it nerves arise, and from them all things of the body. That this is true is proved by dissection. They who know these things, either from the study of anatomical science or from the testimony of those who are skilled in the science, can see that the first principles of life are in the same place as the beginnings of the fibers, and that fibers cannot go forth from themselves, but must go forth from first principles.

These first principles, that is, beginnings, which appear as little glands, are almost countless; their multitude may be compared to the multitude of stars in the universe; and the multitude of fibrils coming out of them may be compared to the multitude of rays going forth from the stars and bearing their heat and light to the earth. The multitude of these little glands may also be compared to the multitude of angelic societies in the heavens, which also are count-

less, and, I have been told, are in like order as the glands. Also the multitude of fibrils going out from these little glands may be compared to the spiritual truths and goods which in like manner flow down from the angelic societies like rays. From this it is that man is like a universe, and like a heaven in least form. From all which it can now be seen that such as life is in first principles, such it is in derivatives; or such as it is in its firsts in the brains, such it is in the things arising therefrom in the body. (Swedenborg, Emanuel, *Divine Love and Wisdom*, 1763, #366, translated by John C. Ager, 1890.)

Chapter 3
CONCEPTUAL BEAUTY:

TRUTH

In the previous chapter, we uncovered enough physical evidence in nature to substantiate the idea that the physical universe was generated from conceptual space by the fractal generator of Divine Love. Galaxies, stars, and planets involved over long ages until earths such as our own manifested all the atomic elements necessary for the generation of organic life. The double-helix DNA molecule was then elaborated over millions of years of evolution on earth. Eventually, a diversity of living organic species evolved in the oceans, the air and the land until natural man (Homo Sapiens) made his appearance on Earth. In other words, man is the harmonic reflection of God; he involved from conceptual space and is evolving or returning to conceptual space (Fig. 3.1). This is essentially why he now possesses a mind to understand Truth and a will to Love.

Fig. 3.1. Involution from Conceptual Space and
Evolution or Return to Conceptual Space

Since physical space must always be in *correspondence* with conceptual space, when this natural involution and evolution took place, corresponding living, mental and emotional energies were being generated within conceptual space. These are the spheres or Heavens of harmonic emotional, mental and vital energy that subsist within our own heart and mind. But what is the form of these Heavens? We have already discovered that galaxy clusters are interconnected in a network that closely resembles the network of neurons of the human brain. This may be a clue. It may be that the macrocosm is organized in accordance with the human structure.

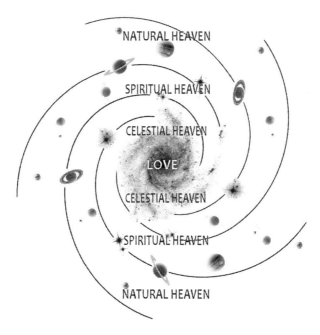

NATURAL HEAVEN

SPIRITUAL HEAVEN

CELESTIAL HEAVEN

LOVE

CELESTIAL HEAVEN

SPIRITUAL HEAVEN

NATURAL HEAVEN

Fig. 3.2. Correspondence between the Physical and Conceptual Heavens

Many of us who have studied human anatomy are amazed by the intricate organization of the human form. For example, the human brain is comprised of about 100 billion neurons and yet this complexity is organized into one whole harmonic neural network. The human respira-

tory, circulatory and digestive systems are equally complex and coherent. And these discrete systems are also
able to interact with each other to keep the human body
alive, healthy and functioning. We know that this human
fractal body did not emerge spontaneously; it took billions of years to evolve. But why would the whole of natural evolution on earth culminate in this human organization? If the physical universe is being generated from
conceptual space by the fractal generator of Divine Love,
the only explanation that seems plausible is that the human form is analogous to the form or structure of Divine
Love. The only difference is that our own human form is finite while Divine Truth must be infinite. And, in fact, Swedenborg was able to confirm this when he was conscious
in the spiritual realm.

Like the human body consists of three main regions,
head, thorax and abdomen, the Heavens of conceptual
space must also consist of three discrete and connected
regions. Swedenborg calls these the Celestial, Spiritual and
Natural Heavens (Fig. 3.2). It would also be reasonable to
speculate that these Heavens must be in correspondence
with God's Love, Wisdom and Power. This is why Heaven
is called the Kingdom of God. Here, we are also able to uncover the real purpose of the universe. The reason the Infinite One or God must generate the universe is to realize
Divine Love. And this purpose must be fully realized in a
harmonic Heaven where God and free, loving and rational
beings (or angels) are conjoined in mutual Love and usefulness.

Since we embed the whole universe within our self, these Heavens must be within us. And we must be returning or evolving into the harmony of Heaven by means of our *will*, *mind* and *life*. This would explain why human beings have developed conscience (harmonic will), reason (rationality) and function (action) (Fig. 3.3). Like our physical body is fractal, our mental and emotional body must be fractal. And these fractals are sustained, maintained and periodically restored by the strange attractor of Love.

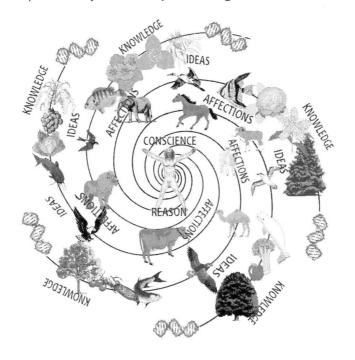

Fig.3.3. Evolution of the Human Mind and Will

The seven days of Creation in Genesis must in fact describe what was occurring in conceptual space when natural evolution was unfolding. The natural evolution of mineral, vegetable and animal life that evolved on planet Earth corresponded to the real knowledge, true ideas and loving affections that evolved within the Heavens of conceptual space (Fig. 3.3). The plants, fish, birds and animals that we see around us in the natural world must correspond to the knowledge, ideas and emotions that we may experience in conceptual space. And, in fact, in the first chapter of Genesis, we read that God or the Infinite One generated man's mind and will in His own image and likeness. We know that God's mind is harmonic mind or Truth and God's will is harmonic will or Divine Love. Hence, the thoughts and emotions that were in the primitive Adamic race must have been rational and innocent just as as the beasts and birds that were around them were gentle, useful and inoffensive:

> And God said, Let the waters bring forth abundantly the moving creature that hath life, and fowl that may fly above the earth in the open firmament of heaven. And God created great whales, and every living creature that moveth, which the waters brought forth abundantly, after their kind, and every winged fowl after his kind: and God saw that it was good. And God blessed them, saying, Be fruitful, and multiply, and fill the waters in the seas, and let fowl multiply in the earth. And the evening and the morning were the fifth day. And God said, Let the earth bring forth the living creature after his kind, cattle,

and creeping thing, and beast of the earth after his kind: and it was so. And God made the beast of the earth after his kind, and cattle after their kind, and every thing that   creepeth upon the earth after his kind: and God saw that it was good.

And God said, Let us make man in our image, after our likeness: and let them have dominion over the fish of the sea, and over the fowl of the air, and over the cattle, and over all the earth, and over every creeping thing that creepeth upon the earth. So God created man in his own image, in the image of God created he him; male and female created he them. And God blessed them, and God said unto them, Be fruitful, and multiply, and replenish the earth, and subdue it: and have dominion over the fish of the sea, and over the fowl of the air, and over every living thing that moveth upon the earth. And God said, Behold, I have given you every herb bearing seed, which is upon the face of all the earth, and every tree, in the which is the fruit of a tree yielding seed; to you it shall be for meat. And to every beast of the earth, and to every fowl of the air, and to every thing that creepeth upon the earth, wherein there is life, I have given every green herb for meat: and it was so. And God saw every thing that he had made, and, behold, it was very good. Genesis 1:20-31.

The Adamic race lived in Goodness and Truth. And we may now also readily understand what the *Garden of Eden* really means. It must be the garden of man's mind when his heart is in innocence (the nakedness of Adam). When our will is in innocence like the heart of the early Adamic race, our mind resembles a beautiful garden filled with elegant plants and flowers (knowledges of Truth), delicious fruit (good works), colorful fish (scientific knowledge), graceful birds (innocent thoughts) and gentle beasts (loving emotions). Truth is conceptual beauty because it represents the graceful, harmonic or rational proportions of Heaven.

Fig. 3.4. The Garden of Eden (Bassano)

In fact, while in the spiritual world, Swedenborg discovered that the soul of animals is in conceptual space:

> No one can know what is the quality of the life of the beasts of the earth, the birds of heaven, and the fishes of the sea, unless it is known what their soul is

and its quality. It is known that every animal has a soul, for they are alive, and life is soul, and this is why they are called in the Word "living souls." That an animal is a soul in its ultimate form, which is corporeal, such as appears before the sight, can be best known from the spiritual world; for in that world, the same as in the natural world, beasts of every kind and birds of every kind, and fishes of every kind, are to be seen and so like in form that they cannot be distinguished from those in our world; but there is this difference, that in the spiritual world they spring evidently from the affections of angels and spirits, so that they are affections made apparent, and consequently they disappear as soon as the angel or spirit departs or his affection ceases. From this it is clear that their soul is nothing else; and that there are given as many genera and species of animals as there are genera and species of affections. (Swedenborg, Emanuel, *Apocalypse Explained* (1757-9), translated by John Whitehead, 1911, #1199)

Our mind must be a fractal because it evolved during millions of years in correspondence with Truth. Conceptual beauty or Truth must be a harmony between conceptual order (unity) and chaos (complexity). Thus, not all thoughts that we presently experience must be beautiful and true. And, if the physical world manifests the realm of our mind and heart, only those species of plants, birds and animals that are beautiful, graceful and useful must represent Truth and Good.

We have seen that plants represent knowledge, fish represent scientific knowledge, birds correspond to thoughts and land animals represent emotions or affections. When we read the first chapter of Genesis, we uncover how God formed the mind of the Adamic race. Owing to the latest discoveries of science, we may also speculate that this early human species may have probably been the Neanderthals, a species which became extinct about 40, 000 years ago. We know that such an early species would certainly have been primitive and ignorant. However, it would be equally reasonable to conjecture that it would have been innocent. This is why we are told that Adam was naked or innocent. Now, what is innocence? Well, if you have ever witnessed the behavior of a three-year old child, you know what innocence is. The mind of such a child is fused with his heart. Children such as these are in a state of ignorance and innocence. They are sincere because their mind is completely harmonized with their heart. This was the state of the Adamic race.

In Genesis 2, we read that Adam names all the birds and animals. What could this mean? In the Bible, to name something is to know its qualities. The DNA of any species is its name. And since animals and birds are affections and thoughts, this could only mean that the Celestial Adamic race intuitively knew what was Good and True because its DNA code was in close correspondence with Divine Love and Wisdom. And the reason these primitive humans instinctively or intuitively understood what was True and Good was because they were innocent. From some of the chaotic behavior we observe in our own times, we can readily conclude that this is certainly not the state of our own being today.

The mind of the Adamic race was like the mind of a very young child. Now, we may think that the mind of such a child is not very intelligent. In fact, the mind of an innocent child is very close to God. When our heart is in innocence, our mind is in spiritual Light or Truth. This is probably why such infants are always smiling. And our own spirit is uplifted into higher states of mind when we see the face of a child. This is also why Swedenborg noticed that some of the highest angels in Heaven, when seen from afar, appear as little children. However, as they approach closer, they manifest as human beings in the prime of life.

We would like to discover the structure of such an innocent mind. And, if what we have previously discussed is true, such a mind should be organized according to harmonic proportions. All the concepts that would be part of such a mind should be fractally organized according to the Golden Spiral. In the Bible, we read that God, before He created birds (thoughts) and animals (affections), brought forth all kinds of plants and trees from the land of the earth. If the land represents our natural self, these plants must be the knowledge that is growing within our mind. In fact, all the beautiful trees, plants, flowers and fruits that we can see in our outer world must correspond to the Truth that may be able to perceive within the conceptual space of our mind.

Natural plants, vegetables and fruits feed our natural body. However, our mind is fed by knowledge and ideas.

The Adamic race was commanded to only eat from the Tree of Life. Therefore, this tree consisted solely of knowledge about what was True and Good. There is an extensive variety of species of plants and flowers on earth because Truth embeds an infinite diversity of concepts within itself. However, only those concepts that are structured harmonically are True. These True ideas or concepts are conjoined with Divine Love. In the realm of mind and ideas, harmony must be synonymous with rationality. Hence, only those concepts that are rational are True. We have seen that Irrational and Transcendental numbers such as π and e are infinitely and fractally rational. Therefore, True concepts must be in harmonic correspondence with the harmonic fractal generator of Divine Love.

Human beings were endowed with rationality in order to understand Truth. When we contemplate all the beautiful and colorful plants, trees, flowers on the Earth, we are seeing the knowledge of Truth manifested physically. Plants are in physical space but knowledge is in conceptual space.

Fig. 3.5. Memory Knowledges of Truth

We know that the physical world consists of material, chemical and biological energy. And each being in this field of energy is a vortex of energy comprised of standing waves. These standing waves are a being's form. And this form is a structure of in-formation. In the case of biological organic beings, such as plants, fish, birds, animals and human beings, this vortex is ingesting waves of energy or food from its environment and digesting them in order to stay alive (keep standing). These waves of energy enter the vortex or stomach of such beings where it is broken down with acids. What is nutritious is then digested by the intestines and metabolized in the liver. And what is not nutritious is eventually evacuated by the colon.

Now, we have already determined that what is in physical space must be in correspondence with what is in conceptual space. Conceptual space consists of emotional, mental and living energy. In this field of conceptual energy, knowledge consists of living energy comprised of standing waves of information. Knowledge of Truth is a conceptual flower, vegetable, or fruit in our mind. When we acquire the knowledge of Truth, we are ingesting a very nutritious living energy. And when we put this Wisdom into practice in our life, we are digesting or incorporating this living energy into our own being or vortex of standing waves. While conscious in the realms of Heaven, Swedenborg perceived many gardens filled with an endless variety of species of plants and flowers because these were outer representations of inner realities of Truth:

> *A certain person who had been much talked of and celebrated in the learned world for his skill in the science of botany, after death heard in the other life,*

to his great surprise, that there also flowers and
trees are presented to view; and as botany had been
the delight of his life he was fired with a desire to see
whether such was the case, and was therefore carried up into the paradisal regions, where he saw
most beautiful plantations of trees and most charming flower gardens of immense extent. And as he
then came into the ardor of his delight from affection, he was allowed to wander over the field, and
not only to see the plants in detail, but also to gather
them and bring them close to his eye, and to examine
whether the case was really so.

Speaking with me from thence he said that he
could never have believed it, and that if such things
had been heard of In the world, they would have
been regarded as marvels. He said further that he
saw an immense abundance of flowers there which
are never seen in the world, and of which it would be
almost impossible there to form any idea; and that
they all glow with an inconceivable brightness, because they are from the light of heaven. That the
glow was from a spiritual origin, he was not yet able
to perceive, that is, that they glowed because there
was in each one of them something of the intelli-

gence and wisdom which are of truth and good. He went on to say that men on earth would never believe this, because few believe there is any heaven and hell, and they who believe only know that in heaven there is joy, and few among them believe that there are such things as eye has not seen, and ear has not heard, and the mind has never conceived; and this although they know from the Word that amazing things were seen by the prophets, such as many things seen by John, as recorded in the Revelation, and yet these were nothing else than the representatives which are continually coming forth in heaven, and which appeared to John when his internal sight was opened. (Swedenborg, Emanuel, *Arcana Coelestia* (1749-56), #4529, translated by John F. Potts, 1905)

In the Bible, the olive tree, the grapevine and the fig tree have important significance. Trees are fractal structures like human beings and societies. All those human beings who love God and obey His laws are like a tree or fractal in conceptual space. But we have uncovered that Heaven consists of three discrete regions that are interconnected. The *Celestial Heaven* is in correspondence with God's Love, the *Spiritual Heaven* with His Truth and the *Natural Heaven* with His Power or Action. In the realm of conceptual plants or knowledge, these three levels correspond respectively to the *olive*, the *grape* and the *fig*.

In the Israelitish church, priests were commanded to anoint kings with olive oil. The lamp in the tabernacle burned with olive oil. Jesus prayed on the Mount of

Olives. Only the five virgins who had (olive) oil in their lamps could enter into the Kingdom of Heaven. Knowing Truth or having faith is important. However, faith without Love is useless because Love is the substance or energy of Truth. Truth is only the form of God's Divine Energy. Hence, kings can only properly govern their kingdom with laws of Truth if they are blessed by God's Love or Divine Energy.

In the Bible, the church is called "a vineyard" because a vineyard is where grapes grow to produce wine. Grapes are the Natural knowledge that can be transformed through fermentation or spiritual temptation into delicious and fortifying wine or Spiritual Truth. Wine must age for a long time before it becomes Good to drink just like we must struggle for many years before we understand Spiritual Truth. Jesus miraculously transformed water or Natural Truth into wine or Spiritual Truth.

Fig. 3.6. Scientific Knowledge

The fig tree is a lowly but wide-spreading tree whose circumference can reach one thousand feet. Thus, unlike the palm, spruce and cypress trees, which are relatively tall, it is very close to the ground. And the ground represents what is natural. Unlike other trees, the fig tree's blossoms tend to be hidden and their fragrance is not readily detectable. The fig tree must represent a knowledge of what is useful in outward life.

In the garden of our mind or conceptual space, the ground or soil represents our natural self where seeds may be planted to produce some Good. Pure water represents natural Truth. A seed of knowledge will not grow without natural Truth or facts. Thus the ocean of natural Truth is filled with conceptual fish or scientific knowledge. Our desire to eat fish in physical space corresponds to our desire for all kinds of scientific knowledge in conceptual space. Many of us are eager to learn about the latest discoveries of science. The incessant movement of fish in the ocean is a physical representation of this desire within us:

"The creatures of the sea" (or fishes) signify knowledges, because the "sea" signifies the natural man, and thus "fishes in the sea" signify the knowledges themselves that are in the natural man. This signification of "fishes" also is from correspondence, for the spirits that are not in spiritual truths, but only in natural truths, which are knowledges, appear in the spiritual world in seas, and when viewed by those who are above, as fishes; for the thoughts that spring from the knowledges with such present that appearance. For all the ideas of the thought of angels and

spirits are turned into various representatives out-
side of them; when turned into such things as are of
the vegetable kingdom they are turned into trees
and shrubs of various kinds; and when into such
things as are of the animal kingdom they are turned
into land animals and flying things of various kinds;
when the ideas of the angels of heaven are turned
into land animals they are turned into lambs, sheep,
goats, bullocks, horses, mules, and other like animals;
but when into flying things they are turned into tur-
tle doves, pigeons, and various kinds of beautiful
birds. But the ideas of thought of those who are nat-
ural and who think from mere knowledges are
turned into the forms of fishes. Consequently in the
seas various kinds of fishes appear, and this it has of-
ten been granted me to see. (Swedenborg, Emanuel,
Apocalypse Explained (1757-9), #513, translated by
John Whitehead, 1911.)

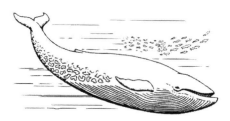

Fig.3.7. Scientific Theory or Principles

Now, whales are a very peculiar kind of fish. First of all,
unlike regular fish, which lay their eggs to reproduce,
whales are mammals that carry their offspring in the

womb. Unlike most fish, which use gills to obtain oxygen from water, whales and dolphins have a spout by which they periodically breathe air. Whales also feed their bodies by ingesting a very large amount of small fish. It seems that whales must represent a special kind of scientific knowledge or Truth. When we have acquired a large amount of scientific facts, we start to organize all these facts and wish to develop a theory that matches the facts as closely as possible. For example, Darwin developed his theory of natural evolution from the scientific facts he gathered during his voyages. In conceptual reality, whales must represent general scientific principles and theories.

In fact, when we start to develop theories or principles from natural facts, we are moving from the sensual knowledge of natural space into the reasoning of conceptual space. We are beginning to breathe air or thought. For hundreds of years, scientists based their knowledge on the facts they obtained using their physical senses and instruments. However, since quantum theory, they have reached a dead end. On the quantum level, physical space, mass, charge and time are absent; only propensities and consciousness remain. Hence, the quantum world is the border between physical and conceptual space. The quantum field of natural Light must be in correspondence with the conceptual field of spiritual Light or Truth. And this Truth is the conceptual form (in-formation) of God's energy or Love. Quantum theory suggests that what we observe is linked to what we think or believe. In fact, scientists are beginning to suspect that all the parts of the universe are interconnected into One Whole. And, moreover, the energy and information of the whole resides in every part.

After He generated whales and fish, God created fowl. In the natural world, these creatures are the birds that roam in the air while, in the conceptual world, they are the thoughts that fly in the conceptual spaces of our mind. When we compare the structure of fish and birds, we notice the similarity (Fig. 3.8). The only difference is that fish have evolved fins to move in the ocean while birds have developed wings to fly in the air. Wings need to be much wider and more muscular because air is less dense than water.

Fig. 3.8. Similarity between Fish and Fowl

When we make any attempt to stop thinking, we notice that it is impossible. It seems that we have absolutely no control of our thoughts; they are incessantly fleeting within our mind like birds. In our case, some of these thoughts may be dark, negative and unpleasant. However, in the case of the Adamic race, which was in innocence, these thoughts must have been true, peaceful, innocent and courageous (Fig. 3.9). Perhaps the most congenial and innocent bird we can find in the natural world is the dove. A dove represents an innocent thought in conceptual space (Fig. 3.10). However, there is an endless variety of charming, colorful and gentle birds that roam the skies of the earth.

Fig. 3.9. True Thoughts

In the Bible, we learn that the Israelites sacrificed many innocent and gentle animals such as lambs and doves in their religious rituals. And, if these physical rituals corresponded exactly to conceptual realities, it would mean that they were offering their innocent emotions and thoughts to God in conceptual space. We also learn that Noah, during the flood, "sent forth a raven, which went forth to and fro until the waters were dried up from off the earth." Since a black raven corresponds to thoughts of ignorance, in conceptual space, it would mean that, after the fall of the Adamic race, man would no longer have direct access to Truth within his mind. Noah knew that the flood was over when a dove he sent out returned with an olive branch. When Jesus was baptized by John the Baptist, we are also told that the Spirit of God descended upon Him like a dove. The Spirit of God is like a dove because God's Truth resembles an innocent thought, a thought that is infinitely harmonized in the Divine Energy of Love.

Fig. 3.10. An Innocent Thought

Now, God's thoughts are not only innocent and pure; they are also all-seeing and powerful. They are like large and powerful eagles that roam the skies and watch over the earth. Eagles have great powers of sight and flight (Fig. 3.11). They can soar into the upper atmosphere with ease. Moreover, they can also detect their preys from very high altitudes and hunt equally well in the air, the sea and the land. Similarly, Divine Truth is omniscient; it can see what is happening in every corner of the universe, from the micro distances of elementary particles, to the lives of minerals, plants, animals and human beings, to the macrocosmic world of planets, stars and galaxies. Divine

Truth can also perceive the form of the future as clearly as the events of the present and the past:

> *For as the heavens are higher than the earth,*
> *so are my ways higher than your ways,*
> *and my thoughts than your thoughts.*
>   Isaiah iv. 9

Fig. 3.11. A Noble and Courageous Thought

The sense of the reality of spiritual things, and the power to rest the thought upon them, is as various as the power of flight in different birds. See a great eagle soaring without effort high in air, or circling with undazzled eyes towards the sun! A noble bird with such powers of flight and of sight pictures an affection for spiritual thought of the strongest, most searching kind, which rises highest above superficial appearances, and takes the most comprehensive views of life, the most in accord with the Divine wisdom.

In Isaiah we read, "They that wait upon the LORD shall renew their strength; they shall mount up with wings as eagles." (Isa. xl. 31) They shall become strong in will for what is good, and shall rise into spiritual intelligence. We can now understand more completely the lament for Saul and Jonathan "They were swifter than eagles, they were stronger than lions." (2 Sam. i. 23) It tells of the spiritual intelligence and the strength which come with the first principles of Divine truth which are adopted to rule the life. Again, "Ye have seen what I did unto the Egyptians, and how I bare you on eagles' wings, and brought you unto myself." (Exod. xix. 4) Power to grasp intellectually spiritual truth, is the means of lifting us up from natural obscurity into heavenly light. Of the Lord's care for His people it is said: "He led him about, he instructed him, he kept him as the apple of his eye. As an eagle stirreth up her nest, fluttereth over her young, spreadeth abroad her wings, taketh them, beareth them on her wings; so the LORD alone did lead him." (Deut. xxxii. 10-12) It tells of the Lord's effort to lift men up to understand spiritual truth in heavenly light, imparting to them of His own Divine intelligence. (Worcester, William L., The Language of Parable, New York, 1892.)

In the course of our life, God's ways may appear to be irrational or bizarre but we should always remember that, in reality, God's thoughts and ways are infinitely rational. The only reason such transcendental ideas and actions may seem strange to our own finite mind is because we are still unable to understand them.

Chapter 4

MORAL BEAUTY:

LOVE

Due to humanity's spiritual downfall, human beings have had trouble discerning the difference between Good and evil. However, as a result of what we have been able to discover in the last chapter, we may be able to understand the nature of real Goodness. If Truth is conceptual beauty and Truth is the form of Love, Love must be moral beauty. When our emotions are organized harmonically, our will has the form of Heavenly Love. Moral Beauty or Love must be a harmony between our own self, the whole universe and God. Emotion is a real and substantial energy that subsists in conceptual space. And, when our will is in accord with Divine Love it becomes harmonic or loving.

We have seen that our own being embeds the whole history of the universe. And our heart or will is a vortex of standing waves of emotional energy. When we freely choose to love all beings unconditionally and unselfishly, and act in accordance with this love, the waves of our being are able to interfere harmonically with all other waves of energy and fractally implode or collapse into the vortex of Divine Love. Hence, our own being becomes the means by which Divine Love is able to re-turn from the material world to Heaven and God.

Since Heaven consists of three discrete regions, the *Natural, Spiritual and Celestial* Heavens, there are essentially three ways that Love can return into Heaven. We can only be conjoined to God through a Life of Useful actions, a Mind of True thoughts and a Will of Good intentions. Those humans who willingly choose to obey God's Heavenly laws enter the *Natural Heaven*. Those who also understand His Truth enter the *Spiritual Heaven*. Finally, those who also intend and do His Loving Will enter the *Celestial Heaven*.

Like we must reason intelligently in order to construct a harmonic or True mind, we must intend and do God's will in order to produce a harmonic or Loving will. The will of the early humans of the Adamic race was innocent or *Celestial* because it was fused with the True form of their mind. Their actions were righteous or True because their will was in accord with the True form of Heaven. Harmony results from Golden Rational Proportions, Hence, the moral law of Heaven must be the Golden Rule. Although each angel or society in Heaven is distinct, separate and different, all these societies and angels are harmonically interconnected according to the Golden Ratio. Therefore, all their thoughts, intentions, emotions and actions interfere constructively or coherently. This Golden arrangement is even perceivable in the plant kingdom on Earth. The leaves in a plant arrange themselves according to phyllotaxis so that every leaf receives as much light from the natural sun as possible. In Heaven, every angel receives as much spiritual Light or Love and Wisdom from the Spiritual Sun (Lord) as possible.

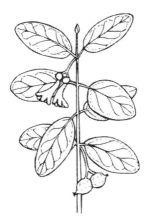

Fig. 4.1. Honeysuckle Plant (Phyllotaxis)

We know that the Golden Rule is "intend and do unto others as you would have them do unto you." Hence, when we are wise, we understand that Love is harmonic reflection. A human being consists of standing waves of energy centered in the freewill of Love. But Love always returns to Love. When we intend, think and act in the world, the waves of our own being proceed out and interfere with all other waves in the universe and then reflect back to us. And, when our intentions are innocent or unselfish, they interfere constructively in the ocean of Love and return to us as more Love in our heart, Truth in our mind and meaningful events in our Life. In contrast, those who disregard the Golden Rule tend to eventually experience the distorted reflection of their selfish intentions as crimes, accidents, confusion and chaos. In the east, this law of spiritual cause and effect is known as *Karma*.

We are also able to visualize the harmony of Love in the harmonic motion and relationship between galaxies, stars and planets. Every cosmic body is gyrating around its own center but it is also harmonically related to all other cosmic bodies. This is well-expressed in Kepler's laws of harmony, especially in Kepler's third law. This law conveys the relationship between each planet and the sun. The ratio of the square of the orbital period of a planet to the cube of its average distance from the sun is identical for all planets (T^2/R^3). And the reason it is identical is because the sun and all planets are interconnected harmonically.

Now, if we assume that a planet's period is its life or action in the world and its distance is its state of being relative to the sun, this would mean that all planets are behaving in perfect harmony with each other and the sun. The planets are moving freely in accordance with harmonic Law. By correspondence, like a planet, our soul should be revolving harmonically around the Spiritual Sun, God or Divine Love. A harmonic will is a will that is in harmony with others and God; it is a will that is acting in accordance with the Golden Rule. Such a will is harmonically conjoined with the Heavens of emotional and conceptual energy through conscience and reason.

Fig. 4.2. The Harmony of the Solar System

Eventually, Newton discovered that this motion of the planets was caused by the law of gravitation and he expressed Kepler's third law of harmony as follows:

$$T^2/R^3 = (4\ \pi^2) / (G\ M_{sun})$$

This ratio is a constant. We also know that Newton's law of universal gravitation can be derived from *the principle of stationary action*. And this action is being propelled by the fractal generator of Divine Love from conceptual space. Hence, the planets are in harmony with Divine Love. Every celestial body is radiating out and gravitating in. And, in order to establish harmony, these two actions must be perfectly balanced. Any excess or lack, either of gravitation or radiation, would produce imbalance. But the harmonic constants of the universe maintain all the parts of the universe in harmonic order.

We have determined that the whole universe is a fractal wave-function of standing waves generated from Divine Love or Divine Energy. Therefore, the universe is not identical with God; it is only His reflected image. The whole universe is a fractal or self-similar image of God. God generates, sustains, maintains and restores the universe by means of the strange attractor of Love. He can even be conjoined with His creation by Love. However, God also remains transcendent and separate from His own creation because He is infinite while the universe and its beings are finite and unbounded. Since our mind and heart are also both finite and unbounded, we can continue to approach God by understanding His Truth and by intending and doing His Love but we can never reach Him. This means that we can continue to be astounded, surprised and delighted by unraveling the infinite mysteries of Love forever, even in the fields of Heaven. This may also be why Heaven is known as the Garden of Delight (Eden).

In physics, we know that standing waves in a medium are produced when the incident waves from a source interfere with the reflected waves emanating from the end of the medium. Now, since God is the Infinite One or the Father of all there is, God's energy or Divine Love must be both the source and the medium. The waves of Love travel until they reach the end of Love. But what is the end of Love? We know that Divine Love is infinite and eternal; it has no end. In Revelation, Jesus says something very strange: "I am the Alpha and the Omega, the First and the Last, the Beginning and the End." We know that Jesus was the Messiah, Christ or the physical manifestation of Love. His own will was the will of God or Divine Love. His will was the beginning or source of Love. But what was He referring to when He said that He was the end of Love? Jesus' physical body was the end of Love. When the waves of Love reach the state of matter, they can only reflect. Hence, matter is the mirror that is able to reflect Love freely. And every physical being is a wave-function of standing waves that is freely reflecting Love. It is equally an interesting fact that a *standing wave* is also called a *stationary wave*. And we have seen that God's action in the universe is *stationary action*. God's action is a harmonic standing wave that generates, maintains and restores harmony everywhere.

We are now in a position to discover what the universe or image of God should be. If Reality is Omnipresent Love, Omniscient Wisdom and Omnipotent action, the substance or energy of the universe must be an image of Divine Love, its form must be an image of Divine Wisdom and its process must be an image of Divine Power or God's action. And the mirror that reflects this image must also consist of three essential components. But these components must not be active; they must be passive or reactive. The reactive component of God's substance (or energy) must be material substance, Matter or physical energy. The reactive component of God's form must be natural form or physical Space. And the reactive component of God's process or action must be Time. This is probably why the physical universe is expanding without bounds and it will take an infinite period of Time to reflect all the infinite qualities of Divine Love.

God's Love, Wisdom and Action should flow into the mirror of Matter, Space and Time and be reflected as a Heaven of Love, Wisdom and Use. This is why Heaven consists of three discrete levels: the *Celestial Heaven* of Love, the *Spiritual Heaven* of Truth and the *Natural Heaven* of Use. Hence, we have a source of Love, Wisdom and Power (God), a mirror of Matter, Space and Time (physical universe) and a reflection or image (Heaven). God continually flows into the universe through correspondence and influx. God is the source of Love, Intelligence and Life which generates, sustains, maintains and heals the universe. And yet, the finite and unbounded universe, which consists both of a material world and a spiritual realm, seems to evolve and exist as of itself because God is also transcendent and infinite.

GOD	MIRROR	REFLECTION	MAN
LOVE	MATTER	CELESTIAL HEAVEN	WILL
WISDOM	SPACE	SPIRITUAL HEAVEN	MIND
POWER	TIME	NATURAL HEAVEN	LIFE

Table 4.1. The Universe as the Self-Similar Image of God

In Genesis, we read that the early Adamic race was generated in the likeness and image of God. The heart or will of these people was filled with loving emotions because it was innocent. Hence, their will was conjoined with God's will or Divine Love. Physically, besides the beautiful plants, fish and birds, the garden or land which they occupied contained certain land animals. These living land animals were closer to their heart than the fish of the sea or the birds of the air. In conceptual space, these land animals represented the loving and innocent emotions or affections of their heart.

Fig. 4.3. Innocent Love

What is the most innocent animal on earth that we can think of? Sheep do not appear to be intelligent nor re-sourceful. They do not even defend themselves when they are provoked and attacked. They also seem not to have a mind or a will of their own because they instinc-tively follow their shepherd. They rely on their shepherd to lead them to green pastures and pure water so they can be properly fed. They are also willing to let others use them as food (meat and milk) and clothing (wool). Their behavior tends to resemble the attitude of infants who are also innocent, helpless and defenseless. And a young sheep or lamb would be even more innocent than an adult (Fig. 4.3).

In the Old Testament, the Israelites not only sacrificed doves; they also sacrificed lambs, kids, rams and bullocks. Sacrifices of lambs were made every Sabbath, new moon and feast. During the Passover feast, every day, a lamb was sacrificed, roasted with fire and eaten. In the New Testament, Jesus is sometimes called "the Lamb of God." Are these all coincidences? No, they are *correspondences*! A lamb corresponds to a feeling of innocence, an emotion that is very close to God or Divine Love.

In Reality, sheep are very wise animals. They are more in touch with the reality of their lives than other cunning beasts. They know that they have nothing of their own and that all that they possess originates from a higher being than themselves. They know that this higher being is more intelligent than they are and he can provide them with all they require for their peaceful existence. They also understand that they must return all this love and care by being loving and useful to others. They do not need to defend themselves because they know that their shepherd will defend them and restore order and justice.

In the whole New Testament, we may readily notice that Jesus never defends Himself, even when He is provoked and attacked. He equally never seeks revenge against His enemies. Even during His last temptation or crucifixion, He makes no attempt to retaliate or escape. Why? His will was the will of God or Divine Love. And Divine Love is completely pure, innocent and unselfish. Yet, Jesus also defended and healed all those who were helpless, defenseless and innocent. This is why He is also called "the Good Shepherd."

> *I am the good shepherd, and I know Mine own, and I am known of Mine. My sheep hear My voice, and I know them, and they follow Me.* John 10:14, 27

Those humans who are in the Love of God follow the Lord like the planets of the solar system harmonically revolve around the sun. But, unlike the planets, humans obey the Lord from the freedom of their own volition. Only what we intend and do from the freedom of our self can become our own. We ARE what we freely love and believe.

Fig. 4.4. The Power of Celestial Love

The people of the Adamic race all had an innocent heart that was conjoined with Divine Love. Now, just because Divine Love is innocent, we should not think that it is powerless. In fact, Divine Love is the most powerful energy in the universe: it is omnipresent, omniscient and omnipotent. This is why Jesus, at other times, is called "the Lion of Judah." In the Old Testament, the tribe of Israel represents the kingdom of Truth and the tribe of Judah refers to the kingdom of Love. These are the two principal kingdoms in Heaven. The lion is known as the king of the animal world because it has no enemies that it cannot readily destroy. By correspondence, God or Divine Love must be the king of our inner or conceptual world (Fig. 4.4):

> Why is the Lord Himself many times called the Lamb? At other times He is called the Lion, to tell us of His Divine courage. What Divine quality is especially suggested when He is called the Lamb? The Divine innocence of His human life, the gentleness, the patience. "Behold' the Lamb of God, which taketh away the sins of the world." (John i. 29) It means that the Lord is innocence itself and that all innocence comes from Him. "He is brought as a lamb to the slaughter, and as a sheep before her shearers is dumb, so he openeth not his mouth." (Isa. liii. 7) The Lord's innocence, and the patience and silence with which He bore temptations, are set before us in this picture. "Blessing, and honor, and glory, and power, be unto him that sitteth upon the throne, and unto the Lamb forever and ever." (Rev. v. 13) He that sitteth upon

*the throne is the Lord; and by the Lamb is meant His
Divine human nature, with special reference to its Divine innocence.* (Worcester, William L., *The Language of Parable*, New York, 1892.)

When our heart is in Celestial Love, we are surrounded
by a field of harmonic emotional energy that is experienced by predators as a blinding light and a tormenting
fire. This field is like the lion's mane or the powerful rays
of the sun. Hence, we have no need to defend ourselves.
When any predator approaches a lion, it does not even try
to attack; it is so awed by the lion's presence and seized
with fear that it readily retreats and escapes. Jesus willingly allowed Himself to be crucified because He was fulfilling
the Scriptures or the Word of God. By undergoing the last
temptation, He fully realized Divine Love and Truth all the
way down to the level of matter. By experiencing the crucifixion, God proved that His Love for the whole human
race is infinite, eternal, unconditional and unselfish. He
also showed us what moral beauty is. In fact, when Peter
tries to defend Him, Jesus says:

*"Put your sword in its place, for all who take the
sword will perish by the sword. Or do you think that
I cannot now pray to My Father, and He will provide
Me with more than twelve legions of angels? How
then could the Scriptures be fulfilled, that it must
happen thus?"* Matthew 16: 52-54

Morality does not pertain to what we are compelled to
intend, think and do. Nobody is forcing us to do anything

because Love is spiritual freedom. No, ethics are concerned with what we should freely intend, think and do
because it is morally beautiful. God gave us the gift of
Love freely and we can only return or reciprocate this
Love freely and willingly. Celestial Love is pure because its
intentions are unselfish. In fact, God generated the universe and its created beings in order to realize His own energy. In order to reflect or reciprocate this Love to the
Creator of the universe as accurately as possible, the intentions of our heart must be as pure, innocent and unselfish as God's Love is towards us. When the waves of energy of our own will are well-intentioned, they are able to
interfere fractally and harmonically and collapse into the
harmonic vortex of Divine Love. Jesus has a more poetic
description of what this means:

> "As the Father loved Me, I also have loved you;
> abide in My love. If you keep My commandments,
> you will abide in My love, just as I have kept My Fa-
> ther's commandments and abide in His love. "These
> things I have spoken to you, that My joy may remain
> in you, and that your joy may be full. This is My com-
> mandment, that you love one another as I have loved
> you. Greater love has no one than this, than to lay
> down one's life for his friends. You are My friends if
> you do whatever I command you. No longer do I call
> you servants, for a servant does not know what his
> master is doing; but I have called you friends, for all
> things that I heard from My Father I have made
> known to you. John 15:9-15

Contrary to conventional opinion, God does want servants; He desires friends in Heaven on which He can bestow His infinite gifts. But, in order to make sure that these friends are true and genuine, God required the material world. Angels must freely evolve as human beings from the material world because this is the only way they are able to reciprocate Love freely and willingly. It is only on the level of material earth that we are able to choose between Truth and falsehood, Good and evil. And it is only what we freely intend, think and do on earth that can become truly own. We are what we freely will, think and do.

Fig. 4.5. Love of Truth

Now, although Love of God (or Good) is the highest degree of spiritual conjunction, we can still be conjoined to God by a Love of Truth or a Love of Neighbor. Unlike sheep, which instinctively follow their shepherd, goats are more inquisitive and independent. They like to wander off and climb on mountains, cliffs and trees in order to explore their environment. Yet, like sheep, goats are also gentle and useful; in fact, they also provide milk, meat and companionship for many people on earth. In conceptual space; goats represent Love of Truth (Fig. 4.5).

We have seen that Wisdom is the harmonic form of Love. This form is infinitely and harmonically proportioned. In fact, many of us love mathematics, art and science because we experience an inner joy from our understanding and creativity. Some of us love to explore the wonders of space, nature, astronomy, the biology of plants, flowers, or the life of reptiles, birds, fish and mammals. Others of us are fascinated by the details and intricacies of the human body or the psychology of the human mind. Some of us love to discover new mathematical or conceptual truths, theorems, equations and theories. Some of us love to use our creative mind to produce artful and useful objects or literary works. Many of us may find enjoyment in studying history, philosophy, theology or religion. Finally, some of us may wish to decipher the meaning of Sacred Scriptures such as the Bible. The joy that we experience from these disciplines always emanates from a pure Love of Truth. In fact, God wants us to understand His Truth. The whole physical universe is a book and every thing in creation is a word in this book. When we discover the spiritual correspondence of any thing, we understand how it fits in the Divine structure and purpose of creation.

It is also reasonable to assume that, if we love Truth, we must also love our neighbor as our self because we know that other beings, minerals, plants, animals and humans are a reflection of the Truth and Beauty that we cherish. We cannot dispute the fact that certain beings in the universe do not reflect Truth and Love as freely and purely as they should. However, we must be patient with the imperfections of others because we are also learning to be human on earth. And the way we learn is by making mistakes and eventually correcting them.

Fig. 4.6. Love of Use

Oxen and cows are also very gentle and useful to human beings; they provide leather, milk and meat for many people all over the world. In the Hindu religion, cows are venerated because they are a symbol of God's plentiful goodness which He bestows upon humans. Due to their strength, patience and bulky stature, oxen also assist some farmers in plowing their soil or pulling heavy loads. Like sheep and goats, they are affectionate towards other members of their herd. However, unlike sheep, which are essentially obedient, oxen tend to be slow and stubborn.

And, unlike goats, they have no desire to explore their environment. When we are neither motivated by Love of Good, nor by Love of Truth, we can still be conjoined with God and Heaven by a Love of Use (Fig. 4.6).

The Kingdom of Heaven is a Kingdom of Use because usefulness is how Love is put into effect. In fact, this is why the physical universe comes into existence. Love has a drive to be useful. And when Love and Wisdom flow into the physical universe, they are realized through usefulness. Without Wisdom, Love would have no form or quality. And without Use, Wisdom would have no actuality. Love is the purpose of the universe, Wisdom is its cause and Use is its effect. The Love of Use is also morally beautiful because it is in harmony with the cause and purpose of creation.

Now, before we end this chapter, there is one last land animal that we should consider. Horses are some of the most beautiful creatures on earth. Their body is mostly muscle and contains almost no fat. Wild horses evolved into existence millions of years ago. And humans started to domesticate horses around 4000 BC. Before the twentieth century and the invention of the automobile, horses were widely used for transportation. Due to their muscle power, they are not only able to trot but also gallop at very high speed, almost in the air (up to 40 mph). The power of locomotion is still expressed today as horsepower because horses are the image of powerful motion.

When we see a horse galloping at such high speed, we are reminded that Divine Love is also a kind of powerful harmonic motion. Since it is in conceptual space, it is a harmonic e-motion. This emotion is organized according to harmonic order or Divine Truth. And this Divine Truth is synonymous with the Word of God. When our heart is in the harmony of Love, we are able to really understand God's Wisdom. And it should not surprise us to learn that, when Swedenborg was conscious in the fields of Heaven, a beautiful white horse was projected in the spiritual atmosphere whenever angels were conversing about the Word of God (Fig. 4.7).

Fig. 4.7. Love and Understanding of the Word

Although they have been widely distorted and corrupted through the passage of time, myths and legends still retain some knowledge and Truth about spiritual reality. For example, Pegasus is a well-known creature in Greek mythology. He is a white stallion with wings (Fig. 4.8). Many Greek poets have written how Pegasus obeyed the Greek God Zeus and ascended into Heaven.

Although there are many stories about Pegasus, he is essentially a symbol of Divine Wisdom and this Wisdom is only contained in God's Word. Swedenborg discovered that this myth is rooted in spiritual correspondence:

> Some weeks later I heard a voice from heaven, saying, "There is another meeting on Parnassus. Come, we will show you the way." I went, and drawing near, I saw a trumpeter on Helicon, announcing and proclaiming the assembly.....

Fig. 4.8. Pegasus

> When the company had climbed the hill Parnassus, some custodians brought water in crystal goblets from a fountain there, and said, "This is water from that fabulous fountain which the ancients said was broken open by the hoof of the horse Pegasus and later consecrated to the nine virgins. By the winged horse Pegasus they meant the understanding of truth, whence is wisdom; by its hoofs, the experiences through which comes natural intelligence; and by the nine virgins, knowledge and information of every kind. These things are called myths today, but

they are correspondences, in the terms of which the early peoples spoke." (Swedenborg, Emanuel, *Conjugial Love*, 1768, Translated by William Wunsch, 1937, #182)

II
HISTORY

Chapter 5

THE FALL OF MAN

In the first section of this book, we discovered that the process of the universe is the harmonic reflection of Divine Love. The universe is being generated, sustained, maintained and restored from conceptual space by the fractal generator and attractor of Love. Beauty is a harmony between Chaos (complexity) and Order (unity) or Freedom and Law. In the material world of our physical body, this beauty is harmonic Life, in the conceptual realm of our mind, it is Truth while, in the moral realm of our will, it is Love. In this section, we are going to explore how the fractal of the universe evolved into what it is at present. And since this fractal is an omnipresent state of energy, we must embed the history of the whole universe as well as the possibilities of its future state within our own being.

Throughout history, time has remained a mystery to philosophers and scientists. Conventionally, time was believed to be how events are ordered. What has already occurred is in the *past*, what is happening now is *present*, and what has yet to be is in the *future*. Such a definition of time would entail that events in the physical world have no sustainability or being. In the physical world, things are be-coming or coming to be but they never are. Scientists in the last few centuries have also defined time as the arrow from order to disorder (Fig. 5.1). In other words, things are always decaying with time. For example, the aging of a biological structure, such as our own human body, is a decaying process. This is otherwise known as the irreversibility of natural processes. According to Big Bang cosmology, as the universe ages, things are becoming disordered. Hence, many scientists predicted the eventual heat death of the universe. Such theories would reduce our life in the universe to a fatal, meaningless and purposeless process.

Fig. 5.1. The Arrow of Linear Time

We can see from figure 5.1 that this is very similar to the order of Natural numbers on the line. But we have already discovered that this order is arbitrary; it is not the reality. Thankfully, owing to Einstein's theory of relativity, ideas about the nature of time began to evolve. We now have a completely different view of the universe. Einstein discovered that the speed of Light is absolute in the physical world and time is relative. Later, Minkowski uncovered that time is the fourth dimension. Physicists then referred to the physical world as spacetime. In his unified field theory, Einstein even conjectured that time is the curvature of space that is caused by the law of universal gravitation. All massive entities are attracted to gravitational centers of mass. However, even today, scientist still do not know where the law of gravitation originates.

Now, all this confusion about the nature of time and the origin of the physical universe can be dispelled when we understand that the physical universe is being generated (or involved) from conceptual space and it is returning (or evolving) to conceptual space. If the velocity of Light is absolute, in the realm of Light, there is no time. In other words, the universe is an omnipresent field of energy. And, if what we have previously conjectured is true, physical energy must be in correspondence with emotional energy. In this omnipresent field of energy, every massive entity is a wave-function of standing waves that reconciles conceptual and physical space. Furthermore, the strange attractor of Divine Love is continually restoring harmony.

Since the universe is a field of physical, vital, mental and emotional energy, it enfolds and embeds all the memories of past events. And, since it is always connected to

the strange attractor of Love, it is equally influenced by
the possibilities of the future state of the universe. In figure 5.2, we can see that, in reality, time must be non-linear
and fractal. Every event leaves its imprint as a memory in
the universal field of energy. These memories are like interference patterns of waves in a hologram. And some humans are even able to retrieve these memories through
conscious perception.

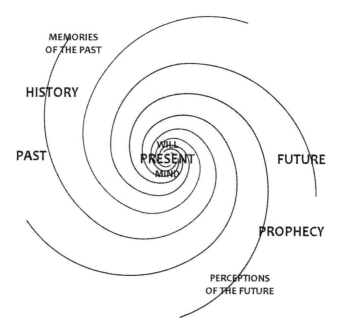

Fig.5.2. The Fractal of Nonlinear Time

We have conjectured that the eternal future of the universe should be a state of universal Love or a Heaven

where God is conjoined with loving and reasonable beings in the Kingdom of Love, Wisdom and Use. This is probably why the Bible contains both the history and prophecy of humankind. However, this does not in any way mean that the future is predetermined. Since the universe is generated by Love, every being in the universe is free to will, desire, think and act as of himself. As living beings become more complex, this freewill increases from minerals, plants and animals until it reaches its peak in man. As a consequence, man is free to obey God's will and reflect Love to Heaven and God or he can refuse to do so and generate his own inner world of selfishness and disorder. Therefore, disorder can and usually does increase on all levels of the universe. However, since all chaos contains the seed of order, when this disorder reaches its maximum point, the strange attractor of Love causes order to emerge from disorder. This is how God heals or restores every process. Through the strange attractor of Love, God is continually guiding all processes into a state of Universal Harmony.

Human beings may deceive and lie but nature does not lie. Thus, we can discover many things about reality by studying the processes of nature. For example, when we study the life of a tree, we begin to understand how every process in the universe involves and evolves with time. Every fruit tree is born from the seed of an older tree that was able to produce fruit. The history and memory of this older tree is embedded within the DNA molecules in the seed. This vital energy enfolds the accumulated heredity, intelligence and evolution of the tree's species. The tree's growth is a seven step process: seed, roots, trunk, branches, flowers and fruits. And we should know by now that this growth is fractal. As it grows and evolves, the tree adapts to its environment, circumstances and climate changes. It needs light from the sun, water and food from the soil to stay alive. Every spring, buds begin to form on the branches and flowers eventually bloom. In summer, under the heat of the sun, the flowers evolve into fruits. In autumn, the leaves change color; they wither and fall. Finally, in winter, the tree becomes completely bare. However, we also know that every winter does come to an end and spring returns. And, from the life of a tree, we may readily detect that the end of any process in nature contains the seed or beginning of a new process .

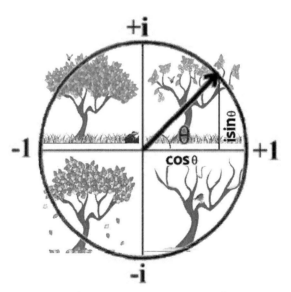

Fig. 5.3. The Process or Seasons of a Tree

Well, the history of humanity is no different. Every civilization, religion or spiritual age in the history of humanity involves and evolves like other processes in nature. Every church or religion is born from the seed or Truth of a previous church. This seed is a vestige of Truth left over from the demise of the previous church. And every religion evolves in time through four changes of state. In the Bible, these states are named: *morning, day, evening and night*. Swedenborg describes these states as (1) a period where Truth is restored, followed by (2) a period of instruction and a time when Truth progresses. When Truth reaches its peak, corruption sets in and (3) a church begins to decline. In the final stage, (4) the church is consummated and devastated of all Good and Truth:

> *In each church there have been four successive changes of states; the first of which was the appearing of the Lord Jehovih and redemption, and then its morning or rise; the second was its instruction and then its midday or progression; the third was its decline, and then its evening or vastation; the fourth was its end, and then its night, or consummation.*
>
> *After its end or consummation the Lord Jehovih appears and executes a Judgment on the men of the former church, and separates the good from the evil, and elevates the good to himself into heaven, and removes the evil from himself into hell.*
>
> *After these things, from the good elevated to himself, he founds a new heaven, and from the evil removed from himself, a new hell; and in both he es-*

*tablishes order, so that they may stand under his aus-
pices and under obedience to him to eternity; and
then through this new heaven he successively inaugu-
rates and establishes a new church on earth.*

*From this new heaven, the Lord Jehovih derives
and produces a new church on earth; which is effected by a revelation from his mouth, or from his Word,
and by inspiration.* (Swedenborg, Emanuel, *Coronis*,
1771, Translated by John Whitehead, 1914, #0)

When we read about the Adamic Church in the first
few pages of the Bible, we notice that there is no mention
of evil or hell. This is because God never generated or created any hell. The creation by God was all Good, True and
Harmonic because it was generated by the harmonic fractal generator of Love. However, we do read that God also
placed the Tree of the Knowledge of Good and Evil in the
garden of man's mind. What does this really mean? If only
the Tree of Life were in man's mind and heart, he would
have no choice; he would be compelled to love God like
an automaton or robot. In order to reciprocate Love
freely, willingly and reasonably, man must be free and
able to choose.

Now, although the Adamic people knew what was
Good and True intuitively, they began to desire what was
their own. It is obvious that man's own or his natural self
is nothing but an empty recipient that can only receive
and reflect Divine Love. But we can notice this same behavior in young children who sooner or later desire to exercise their freewill and no longer wish to obey their par-

ents. In order to make this possible without causing further damage to man's soul, God put Adam into a deep sleep. Spiritual sleep is a state of forgetfulness where we forget that we are connected and sustained by God. Many of us are still in this state of hypnosis. We may be physically awake but we are spiritually asleep. Hence, most of us still believe that we possess our own intelligence and power. If we were to awaken from this sleep we would realize that any intelligence, love and power that we may have is flowing into us from God because God is the only self-existent source of Love, Wisdom and Power in the universe.

We then read that God brought forth Eve from Adam's rib. Adam's rib cage encases his living heart and lungs. But his ribs are relatively dead bones. Thus, Eve was man's projected self. By loving his wife or spouse, man is able to love himself in another. The soul of the Adamic race was still spiritually alive because real marriage love is synonymous with Celestial Love. But we know that the problems really started when Eve met the serpent in the garden. At that time, like all animals in the Garden of Eden, the serpent was not poisonous. In conceptual space, the serpent corresponds to the love of what is sensual because a snake is all feet and crawls and slithers on the ground. The Adamic race certainly possessed physical senses like all human beings. But the spiritual fall starts when we begin to only believe what our physical senses tell us.

We read that Eve was tempted by the serpent to eat from the Tree of Knowledge of Good and Evil. When we exist in the physical world, our sensual mind deceives us by telling us that the material world is reality. The serpent also says to Eve that if she eats from this tree that "...ye shall be as gods knowing good and evil." This may be relatively factual but the serpent, or our sensual mind, is also cunning and deceitful. This is why this lower mind intentionally fails to mention that, by becoming a god in our own mind, we also generate our own hell. Hence, here we discover that it was man who generated his own hells.

We have already seen that the universe was initially generated by Divine Love. This means that Love is able to create. And since humans were endowed with freewill, they can exercise this creative ability by cooperating with God, by believing what is True, intending what is Good and doing what is Useful. However, when man believes what is false and intends and does what is evil or selfish, he begins to generate mental and emotional fields that are disordered. These dark worlds of fantasy, lies, selfishness, greed, fear, hatred and cruelty subsist outside of Heaven, although they are kept somewhat alive by certain emanations from Heaven.

There can only be One God in the universe and that God is Divine Love. When we love, believe and obey this One God, our will and mind subsist in the reality of Heaven or the Kingdom of God. However, when we love our own self and the world, we subsist in the fantasy of our own imagination and the selfishness of our heart; we in effect subsist in our egocentric hell. Hence, this is how the Adamic Church began to fall from spiritual Light into the darkness of its own imagination:

Because thou hast hearkened unto the voice of thy wife, and hast eaten of the tree, of which I commanded thee, saying, Thou shalt not eat of it: cursed is the ground for thy sake; in sorrow shalt thou eat of it all the days of thy life; Thorns also and thistles shall it bring forth to thee; and thou shalt eat the herb of the field... Genesis 3:18-19

When we read these words, it appears as though God is chasing us out the Garden of Truth and Love. However, the literal sense of the Bible is always describing how things appear to the human race depending on its inner state, very much like the sun appears to rise and set because we exist on the Earth and the Earth is spinning. Similarly, when we generate our own hell of self-love and self-intelligence, it appears as though God is judgmental and cruel. In reality, God is always merciful and continually shining His Light, Truth and Love upon the human race:

He maketh his sun to rise on the evil and on the good, and sendeth rain on the just and on the unjust. Matthew 5:45

Thus began the spiritual fall of man. When we are in self-love and self-intelligence, we lose all Good and Truth; we generate falsehoods and we must survive on a lower form of knowledge. Adam and Eve or the Adamic race was no longer innocent (naked); it began to be ashamed and it covered itself with fig leaves (natural knowledge). This is the guilt or shame that still persists within man's heart. From that fateful day in the history of humanity, hell began to be generated in the collective field of human vital, mental and emotional energy. Hence, the spiritual or conceptual world of man now consists of both Heaven and hell separated by an intermediate region or a state of spiritual equilibrium where we are still able to choose between Truth and falsehood, Good and evil, Heaven or hell.

The Bible speaks a great deal about man's salvation and damnation because it encapsulates the Truth regarding our history as well as our future state. The Bible is the Word of God or Truth because it concerns God's relationship with humanity. But why would this Truth be contained in a book of strange stories that hardly make any sense. It is because the Bible was written by means of the *science of correspondences*. These are the same correspondences that we have discovered between physical and conceptual space. In fact, the Adamic race had no need for a Word because it had direct Celestial perception. However, after humanity continued to fall, a written Word was eventually required to keep humanity connected with Heaven and God:

> *I have been told from heaven that the most ancient people, because their interiors were turned heavenwards, had direct revelation, and by this means there was at that time a conjunction of the Lord with the human race. After their times, however, there was no such direct revelation, but there was a mediate revelation by means of correspondences, inasmuch as all their Divine worship then consisted of correspondences, and for this reason the churches of that time were called representative churches. For it*

was then known what correspondence is and what representation is, and that all things on the earth correspond to spiritual things in heaven and in the church, or what is the same, represent them; and therefore the natural things that constituted the externals of their worship served them as mediums for thinking spiritually, that is, thinking with the angels.

When the knowledge of correspondences and representations had been blotted out of remembrance a Word was written, in which all the words and their meanings are correspondences, and thus contain a spiritual or internal sense, in which are the angels; and in consequence, when a man reads the Word and perceives it according to the sense of the letter or the outer sense the angels perceive it according to the internal or spiritual sense; for all the thought of angels is spiritual while the thought of man is natural. These two kinds of thought appear diverse; nevertheless they are one because they correspond. Thus it was that when man had separated himself from heaven and had severed the bond the Lord provided a medium of conjunction of heaven with man by means of the Word. (Swedenborg, Emanuel, *Heaven and Hell*, 1758, Translated by John C. Ager, #306)

In figure 5.4, we can see that the Word of God itself is a strange attractor. This strange attractor is always restoring harmony. In the first verse of John, we read that "In the beginning was the Word, and the Word was with God and the Word was God." We know that God is Divine Love but this Love is infinitely and harmonically organized in the form of Truth which is the Word of God. In conceptual space, this Truth is the rational organization of our mind or Heaven. However, in the physical world, this Word or Truth is also manifested as the Bible.

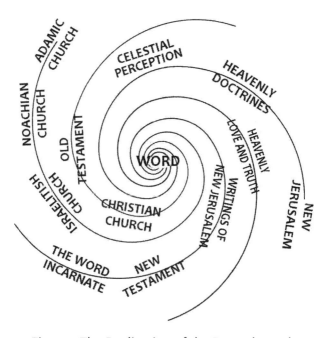

Fig. 5.4. The Realization of the Eternal Word
in History and Prophecy

Since the written Word descends from Heaven, it has a different meaning on each level of Heaven. And since Heaven is in the conceptual space of our mind, when we understand the meaning of the Word, we are automatically affiliated with the corresponding societies of angels in Heaven. The Word is in fact the means by which we can be conjoined with Heaven and God. The *Natural* or literal meaning contains the history and prophecy of human spiritual evolution. The *Spiritual* meaning embodies the knowledge we require to redeem our soul and return into the Holy fields of Heaven. And the *Celestial* sense holds information regarding God's incarnation as the Messiah on earth. It clearly depicts how He redeems the collective field of human energy and restores spiritual equilibrium by resisting human temptations. Before this critical event occurred, it was a prophecy in the Old Testament, but after it unfolded, it became a historical event and memory embedded within the collective consciousness of humanity as well as a story recorded in the Sacred Scriptures of the New Testament.

The first Biblical flood was the end or consummation of the Adamic Church. Since water corresponds to Truth, in conceptual space, when this Truth is perverted, it becomes a torrent of falsehood. This is usually what happens at the end of a spiritual age: the mind of man degenerates into chaos. But we know that chaos always contains the seed of a new order. Noah was a man who walked with God. Hence, Noah becomes the seed of the next church. Noah's ark is the mind of man. Like Heaven, this ark or mind consists of three levels: the *Celestial*, *Spiritual* and *Natural*. And we are told that Noah is commanded by God to fill the ark with pairs of all species of animals, male (understanding) and female (will). Thus, in order to save or redeem humanity from its spiritual fall, God needed to separate man's will from his understand-

ing. In the Noachian Church, man would no longer perceive Truth directly or intuitively. Instead, he would need
to understand Truth with his mind.

Fig. 5.5. The Ankh or Key of Life

Ancient Egypt was probably such a civilization because
at its outset it arose from a monotheistic religion. All
Egyptian symbols, pictographs and hieroglyphics represented conceptual realities. And the early Egyptians were
able to decipher the meaning of these symbols by means
of the *science of correspondences*. In fact, the knowledge
of astrology that we have today is the frail remnant of this

ancient and accurate science. The various gods and goddesses depicted in Egyptian art actually refer to various qualities of the One and Only God. The Egyptian symbol of the Ankh is also a strange mixture between the circle of eternity and the Christian cross of spiritual temptation (Fig. 5.5). To the Egyptians, it was known as the Key of Life. It may have also been a prophetic symbol of what would eventually occur in the future.

In the beginning, the ancient Egyptians must have known that God was One, Holy and Infinite because the very definition of God is Infinite Oneness. And a kingdom with many gods or rulers becomes chaotic, as in hell where there are many devils who desire to control each other through threat, fear and punishment. Hence, when this civilization deteriorated, these people began to worship the gods, goddesses and statues themselves and they started to misuse and abuse the *science of correspondences* by practicing magical arts. And what began as a monotheistic religion degenerated into polytheism, idolatry and magic. In the story of the tower of Babel, we are told how the Noachian age ended when God confounded their mind and scattered them over the face of the earth.

We can begin to see how the fractal history of the universe is unfolding and enfolding. The Word is becoming increasingly complex and material. Now, when the Noachian Church was devastated of all Good and Truth, God needed to restore the symbols and sacred rituals of religion in order to keep mankind connected to the Heaven of conceptual reality. Thus, the Israelitish Church was born from the ashes or chaos of the Noachian Church.

This church consisted of many religious rituals and a written Word elaborated from the Ten Commandments, which Moses received on mount Sinai, and the revelations obtained by the major and minor prophets of Israel.

The Old Testament includes the history of previous churches which Moses obtained from the Ancient Word. It also encloses the history of the Israelitish Church, from its beginning to its final demise and devastation. On the *Spiritual* level, this history is also a parable of the evolution of the human heart and mind. Hence, the Bible is essentially a spiritual manual that we may use and apply to transform our life, mind and heart. This is how God is able to reform our mind, regenerate our will and save our soul by means of His Word. God speaks to us through His Word.

The Israelitish Church began with the call of Abram. Abram was the seed of Truth of the Israelitish Church. And, when Abram and Sarai were very old (wise), God appeared to Abram and made a covenant with him:

> *And when Abram was ninety years old and nine, Jehovah appeared to Abram, and said unto him, I am God Almighty; walk before me, and be thou perfect. And I will make my covenant between me and thee, and will multiply thee exceedingly. And Abram fell on his face: and God talked with him, saying, As for me, behold, my covenant is with thee, and thou shalt be the father of a multitude of nations. Neither shall thy name any more be called Abram, but thy name shall be Abraham; for the father of a multitude of nations*

have I made thee. And I will make thee exceeding fruitful, and I will make nations of thee, and kings shall come out of thee. Genesis 17:1-6

Fig. 5.6. High Priest and Sacred Rituals
of the Israelitish Church

We can readily notice in the Bible that, when any radical spiritual transformation occurs in the collective consciousness of humanity, God modifies a person's name to reflect this change. This is because, in conceptual reality, a person's name represents his qualities, just as his DNA represents his blueprint in physical reality. In fact, by

changing our spiritual qualities through spiritual transformation, we can modify our DNA and heal.

This covenant with Abraham was symbolized by the rit-
ual of circumcision which is still practiced today. The
removal of the foreskin in male children represented the
removal of all impurities that were defiling Celestial Love
because the human reproductive organs and marriage
Love also correspond to Celestial Love. And, although the
Israelites practiced these sacred rituals and strictly
obeyed all the commandments, they did not understand
their conceptual or Heavenly meaning. In the Israelitish
Church, the Word had reached the *Natural* level and the
Israelites only understood the Word literally.

After the covenant was made, Sarai's name is transformed into *Sarah* and she is able to give birth to a son
Isaac. Unlike Ishmael's birth, which resulted from a bond-
servant, Isaac's birth represents the birth of True rationality in the human mind. But freedom and rationality can
only be realized or put into effect in the natural world.
Isaac and Rebekah give birth to twins. Whenever we encounter twins in the Word, they usually refer to the two
essential qualities of the human soul: *will* and *understanding*. For example, Adam and Eve's twins, Cain and Abel,
represented the two main sects in the Adamic Church,
those who were driven by faith (Cain) and those who
were motivated by Love or charity (Abel). When Abel is
killed by Cain, faith loses its vital energy. Isaac's twins, Jacob and Esau, represent natural Truth and Good. Before
we are able to perform Good works instinctively from the
joy of our heart, we must first imitate Esau by artificially

obeying the laws of Truth. This is why Jacob steals Esau's birthright by deceiving his father Isaac.

Jacob's name is transformed into Israel when he wrestles all night with an angel and is finally blessed by God. Jacob has 12 sons which become the twelve tribes of Israel. Like the numbers 3 and 7, the number 12 is prevalent in the pages of the Bible. Twelve is the product of three multiplied by four. According to Swedenborg , "the number *three* signifies everything as to truth, and the number *four* everything as to good; hence *twelve*, in this instance, signifies everything as to truth from the good of love." This is also why the High priest in the Israelitish Church wore a breastplate decorated with *twelve* precious stones arranged according to Divine Order (Fig. 5.6).

Joseph and Benjamin are Jacob's favorite sons. And Jacob gives Joseph a coat of many colors (qualities of Truth). Furthermore, Joseph relates a dream to his brothers in which he is exalted above them. The brothers become jealous and decide to sell him as a slave. In Egypt, Joseph is imprisoned with two criminals: a butler (understanding) and baker (will). When Joseph interprets Pharaoh's dream, the king frees him and makes him his adviser. Joseph preserves the wheat in Egypt and eventually reconciles with his brothers.

Now, many people wonder why the Bible contains these extremely detailed, personal and accurate stories regarding the history of the Israelites. And the only explanation for this is that, on the *Spiritual* level, these stories correspond exactly to what occurs within the human soul during man's spiritual evolution. As we can readily deduce, the human mind must first go down to Egypt or the *Natural* level before it can be raised again into the harmonic fields of Heaven.

Three hundred years pass by and the Israelites are taken as slaves in Egypt to build the Egyptians' monuments and statues. This outer slavery corresponds to man's inner slavery when he is ruled by his own natural ego (Pharaoh). But two Levites have a son (Moses). His mother places him in a basket on the Nile river where he may be retrieved by Pharaoh's daughter. Hence, Moses, an Israelite, is raised as an Egyptian. When Moses sees an Egyptian mistreat a Hebrew slave, he kills him. Moses is then forced to flee the Egyptians and live among the Israelites.

Now, most of us are very familiar with the story of Moses and the Israelites. But what does it all represent in conceptual space? Once again, Moses is the seed of Truth that germinates in the chaos of our natural mind (Egypt). Moses sees God in an eternally burning bush. In conceptual space, a bush or plant is knowledge, fire is the heat or energy of Love. The knowledge of the Word contains the power of Divine Love within it. Moses receives the tablets engraved with the Ten Commandments on mount Sinai (a state of higher Love). We also learn that God commands Moses to build the ark of the covenant in order to preserve the stone tablets. The ark was to be made of acacia wood (rationality), 2.5 cubits long, 1.5 cubits wide and 1.5 cubits high, overlaid with pure gold. The mercy seat, which was above the ark, was to be constructed of solid gold. And Moses was commanded to obtain this gold from the jewelry of the Israelites. Once again, this is all very precise. In fact, like the covenant of circumcision with Abraham, Moses was to build a symbolic attractor that would conjoin the Israelites to Heaven and restore or heal their soul.

Spiritual gold corresponds to Love because Love is the most precious substance in Heaven. The ark was to be constructed according to the Golden Ratio. 2.5 cubits divided by 1.5 cubits (1.666..) is approximately equal to φ = 1.618... (Fig. 5.7). The two angels represent the union of Truth and Good, Wisdom and Love, will and understanding, involution and evolution, love of Good (God) and Love of Truth (neighbor).

Fig. 5.7. The Ark of the Covenant

Now, we may also notice that, even though the human race continues to fall spiritually, it is nevertheless kept connected to Heaven by the spiritual attractor of Love. Moses and Aaron eventually die and are replaced by Joshua and Eleazar. Unlike Moses who was a leader that represented the Law or Word, Joshua was a warrior. All these Biblical persons represent the Lord within us who is always fighting for our salvation. Joshua leads the children of Israel into the promised land. We read that he destroys the walls of Jericho by means of the sound of trumpets. Like all Biblical tales, this may seem very strange. However, these stories always refer to scientific realities. When we understand that all objects in the material world are standing waves of energy, this story begins to make sense. When we know the dominant frequency of any entity, we have the key to its internal structure. And we may readily destroy it by means of harmonic resonance. For example, we can shatter a glass by sounding its resonant note. In conceptual space, the standing waves of our being represent our conceptual form or belief system. And when we discover the dominant frequency of our ruling love, we have the key to our spiritual transformation. This is the key that opens the door to Heaven.

Joshua eventually conquers the land and distributes it among the twelve tribes. However, after Joshua's death conflict between the tribes ensues as well as disorder and corruption. We have already seen that Freedom and Law are intrinsically related. In the physical world, in order to establish a stable, free and civil society, we require one ruler (king) and civil laws. In the conceptual space or the kingdom of our mind, we also require a single ruler or spiritual King. The Israelites prayed for a king. And Hannah gave birth to a special child, Samuel. In the Bible, God's Love is represented by priests or prophets and His Wisdom or Law is personified by a king. Samuel was the prophet sent by God to seek and identify the first three kings of Israel: Saul, David and Solomon. Once again, these three kings and their respective reigns represent our spiritual journey through the *Natural*, *Spiritual* and *Celestial* states of the human mind.

As we have seen, the land we possess always corresponds to our state of being. And, in order to move into a new land, we must first conquer the enemies which occupy it. These spiritual enemies are the false thoughts and selfish lusts that reside in the conceptual spaces of our mind and heart. Since Saul represents the *Natural* level of our mind, the reign of Saul is characterized by conflict, violence and war. And Saul is not always victorious over his enemies because, on the *Natural* level, we only obey God's Laws out of fear of the consequences and, whenever we perform any righteous or good action, we tend to attribute all merit to ourselves.

Samuel must eventually search for a new king. Unlike Saul, David was a shepherd who played the harp. And we have discovered that sheep represent innocent Love. When we have the Love of Truth within our heart, we are protected by the shield of Love and we can fight the enemy with the sword of Truth. Hence, David is able to destroy the giant Goliath (self-pride and self-intelligence) by means of a few stones (Truths) from the brook (Word). Although David is far from perfect, he is the beloved of God because all his intentions and actions are heartfelt sincere and genuine. And, when he is anointed king, he continues to fight wars but, unlike Saul, he is always victorious. When we are on the *Spiritual* level, we perform good and righteous actions from the love of Truth in our heart and attribute all the merit to God. During his whole reign, king David longs to build a permanent temple for the Lord like we desire to find the Peace of God in our own heart.

It is only in the reign of David's son Solomon (Peace) that a permanent temple for God is built. Hence, Solomon reaps the fruit of David's hard fought battles and wars. And we read that, during Solomon's reign, there is an abundance of gold (Love) in the land. When we enter the *Celestial* state, our mind is at peace and our heart is in Love. However, once again, as Solomon's reign approaches its end, we read that the king had many concubines and, instead of worshiping the One True God, he begins to worship idols and statues. The kingdom becomes divided into Judah and Israel. This type of division is still present today. There is a division between those who are affectionate and those who are intellectual. And this is reflected in the way they worship God.

Thus the kings that followed Solomon's reign were all divisive and the sects and kingdoms that were formed only produced more confusion, injustice and chaos among the people. This is how the history of the Israelitish Church ended. We read that there was famine in the land which means that the spiritual Goods and Truths from Heaven were no longer able to flow by correspondence into the material level of Earth. However, we now know that Chaos always contains the seed of Order. In this instance, these seeds of Truth and Good are the major and minor prophets of the Old Testament. Most prominent among these were Elijah, Jeremiah, Isaiah, Ezekiel and Daniel. These prophets began to preach the end and devastation of the Israelitish Church:

And now, O inhabitants of Jerusalem and men of Judah, judge, I pray you, betwixt me and my vineyard. What could have been done more to my vineyard, that I have not done in it? wherefore, when I looked that it should bring forth grapes, brought it forth wild grapes? And now I will tell you what I will do to my vineyard: I will take away the hedge thereof, and it shall be eaten up; I will break down the wall thereof, and it shall be trodden down: and I will lay it waste; it shall not be pruned nor hoed; but there shall come up briers and thorns: I will also command the clouds that they rain no rain upon it. Isaiah 5: 3-6

And when I shall extinguish thee, I will cover the heavens, and make the stars thereof dark; I will cover the sun with a cloud, and the moon shall not give its light. All the bright lights of heaven will I make dark over thee, and set darkness upon thy land, saith the Lord Jehovah. I will also vex the hearts of many peoples, when I shall bring thy destruction among the nations, into the countries which thou hast not known. Ezekiel 7-9

As we read these words, once again, we should realize that this is how God's judgment appears to us when we continue to live in sin. The end, consummation and devastion of the Israelitish Church was probably the worst and darkest period in the history of humanity because the Word had become completely material and only falsity and evil remained. It was a much worse situation than we are experiencing today. At that time, the evil from hell had become so prevalent that some people were possessed by evil spirits. And, as the evil from hell was let loose, evil spirits were also threatening to disturb the intermediate realm of spirits and the harmonic order of Heaven. However, as we can readily notice from the diagram of figure 5.4, this was a part of the greater plan. The Word needed to fall all the way down to the level of matter or spiritual darkness before it could be raised by the Lord.

Now, although the Hebrew prophets preached the end of the Israelitish Church, they also rekindled hope and faith in the hearts of the people by foretelling the coming of the Messiah on earth. Through His incarnation as Jesus the Messiah on Earth, God would again implant the seeds of Truth in the hearts of the people and begin to raise the Word into Heaven. In subsequent chapters, we will discover how God was able to accomplish this Divine Operation and raise the Christian Church. We will also unveil how this Christian Church also degraded into the state that we find it today.

The prophecies about the coming of the Messiah on Earth are well-documented in the Old Testament as well in more ancient Scriptures such as the myth of Osiris in Egyptian culture. And it is rather astonishing that the Elders of the Jewish Church would eventually reject Jesus. However, this behavior by the Jewish establishment was also prophesied in the Old Testament itself. Jesus was well-aware of this when He said that He came to fulfill the Scriptures. The latter part of the Old Testament is replete with these prophesies by the major and minor prophets of Israel:

BEHOLD, I will send my messenger, and he shall prepare the way before me: and the LORD, whom ye seek, shall suddenly come to his temple, even the messenger of the covenant, whom ye delight in: behold, he shall come, saith the LORD of hosts. Malachi 3

Therefore the Lord himself will give you a sign: The virgin will conceive and give birth to a son, and will call him Immanuel. Isaiah 7:14

BEHOLD, The sceptre shall not depart from Judah, nor a lawgiver from between his feet, until Shiloh come; and unto him shall the gathering of the people be. Genesis 49: 10

But thou, Bethlehem Ephratah, though thou be little among the thousands of Judah, yet out of thee shall he come forth unto me that is to be ruler in Israel; whose goings forth have been from of old, from everlasting. Micah 5: 2

Rejoice greatly, O daughter of Zion; shout, O daughter of Jerusalem: behold, thy King cometh unto thee: he is just, and having salvation; lowly, and ridingupon an ass, and upon a colt the foal of an ass. Zechariah 9: 9

Then the eyes of the blind shall be opened, and the ears of the deaf shall be unstopped. Isaiah 5:5

I will declare the decree: the Lord hath said unto me, Thou art my Son; this day have I begotten thee. Psalms 2: 7

And I said unto them, If ye think good, give me my price; and if not, forbear. So they weighed for my price thirty pieces of silver. Zechariah 11:12

Seventy weeks are determined upon thy people and upon thy holy city, to finish the transgression, and to make an end of sins, and to make reconciliation for iniquity, and to bring in everlasting righteousness, and to seal up the vision and prophecy, and to anoint the most Holy. Daniel 9: 24

They part my garments among them, and cast lots upon my vesture. Psalms 22:18

But he was wounded for our transgressions, he was bruised for our iniquities: the chastisement of our peace was upon him; and with his stripes we are healed. Isaiah 53: 5

For dogs have compassed me: the assembly of the wicked have inclosed me: they pierced my hands and my feet. Psalms 22:16

And I will pour upon the house of David, and upon the inhabitants of Jerusalem, the spirit of grace and of supplications: and they shall look upon me whom they have pierced, and they shall mourn for him, as one mourneth for his only son, and shall be in bitterness for him, as one that is in bitterness for his firstborn. Zechariah 12: 10

He keepeth all his bones: not one of them is broken. Psalms 34:20

But God will redeem my soul from the power of the grave: for he shall receive me. Psalms 49:15

Chapter 6

NATURAL ORDER
AND DISORDER

In the last chapter, we detected that, when the human race fell spiritually, it began to generate disordered conceptual fields or hells that are not in accord with the will of God or Divine Love. And, since Love or freewill is creative, the evil affections and false ideas that comprised these fields began to manifest as natural disorder on earth. This is probably why we can presently witness both order and disorder on the physical level. This disorder can be found in all domains of life on earth, on the mineral, vegetable, animal and human levels.

Since all things in the universe are interconnected by Love, Wisdom and Use, all things are interdependent. Hence, the well-being of any one thing is completely dependent upon the well-being of the whole. We have seen how this symbiosis or interdependence is expressed in the harmony of Heaven, the human body as well as in other wholesome and healthy organisms. However, when hell manifests on the natural level, it can only display selfish, turbulent and distorted forms and events.

Fig. 6.1. Tornado

When the spiritual Goods and Truths of Heaven are no longer able to flow by correspondence and influx into the natural level of earth, this lack of order and harmony usually manifests as floods, droughts, fires, earthquakes, storms, hurricanes, tsunamis and tornadoes. This is because what occurs in the natural atmosphere corresponds to what is happening in the conceptual and emotional atmosphere. Such extreme physical events usually unfold at the end of a spiritual age. But we can equally witness such turbulence on a lower scale in our everyday existence. For example, there is a time of the year when tornadoes and hurricanes are prevalent (Fig 6.1). Now, although the climate and weather on earth are chaotic and fractal as well as difficult to predict, they are still subject to universal laws. And, when storms reach their peak, the fractal at-tractor of Love is able to restore order, harmony and peace in the natural atmosphere.

When man's mind was in the Garden of Eden, there were only beautiful trees, plants flowers and fruits on earth. However, when man fell from innocence, the ground of his own being became "cursed" and it brought forth "thorns and thistles."   Many flowers and plants, such as roses, use thorns as a defense mechanism. How-ever, when a plant consists almost wholly of thorns, it becomes useless and hurtful to its environment (Fig. 6.2). This corresponds to a kind of selfishness and a lack of co-operation in the human mind.

Fig. 6.2. Thistle

Today, we not only witness beautiful and fragrant plants and flowers on earth, we can also find useless and noxious plants such as poison ivy. Some of these plants tend to emanate putrid odors. For example, the titan arum, also known as the "corpse flower," is an abnormal-ly large plant that can reach up to 10 feet (Fig. 6.3). It also emanates the smell of rotten meat or dead animals. This foul odor attracts all kinds of insects which facilitate its pollination.

Fig. 6.3. Titan Arum (Amorphophallus Titanum)

In chapter 2, we already encountered the arum flower. However, unlike the titan arum, it was harmonically proportioned and agreeably linked to the rest of its environment; its colors were lovely and its odor was fragrant. From disorder in the plant kingdom, we can then conclude that evil, instead of generating what is in harmony with the whole, selfishly generates what profits its own self. Hence, the natural forms that result from evil tend to be distorted, perverted and excessive. It is also interesting that Swedenborg detected that evil spirits are attracted by foul odors in the spiritual world:

When the truths and goods of faith are destroyed and thus obstructed, they are then represented by foul odors, like those of ponds and dead bodies; this is also the case if it happens owing to man's plea-sures. (Swedenborg, Emanuel, *Spiritual Experiences* (1765), #201, translated by J. F. Buss)

Since harmonic plants and flowers correspond to all kinds of knowledge and especially knowledge of Truth, in conceptual space, unsightly, poisonous, thorny, stinking and noxious plants and flowers must correspond to a knowledge that is false or distorted.

Fig. 6.4. Hammerhead Shark and Sawfish

We have seen that there are countless species of pleas-ant and colorful fish in the sea. Even relatively large species such as dolphins and whales are gentle and inoffensive. Such species do eat other fish to survive but their own existence is in symbiosis with the rest of their oceanic environment. However, in the vastness of the ocean we also encounter species that are rather greedy and cruel such as sharks, sawfish and octopi. These species seem to have evolved organs that are not very graceful. For example, the hammerhead shark and sawfish in figure 6.4 seem particularly grotesque and monstrous.

Fig. 6.5. Frog

One of the least graceful species of animals in nature is the frog (Fig. 6.5). In fact, in many fairy tales, the handsome prince is sometimes magically transformed into an ugly frog. Frogs are carnivorous amphibians with protruding eyes and cleft tongue. Their skin is glandular and it often secretes toxic substances. When Pharaoh refused to liberate the Israelites, the Egyptians were cursed with many plagues, one of which was the plague of frogs. Such hideous creatures correspond to reasonings that arise from falsities. In this case, frogs were an outer manifestation of the Egyptians' inner distorted state of consciousness. Hence, it is always our own inner disorder which generates the chaos that we experience outwardly.

God only generates what is Good and True and restores harmony everywhere because His form is Divine Order itself.

Most reptiles, such as alligators, turtles, lizards and snakes are characterized by their thick and callous skin or their outer shells. These creatures have been able to survive in harsh, and extreme environments such as deserts and swamps. Such cruel reptiles as dinosaurs already roamed the earth millions of years ago. These creatures eventually became extinct when conditions on earth were more conducive for the evolution of gentler animal species and warm-blooded mammals.

Fig. 6.6. Poisonous Snake

The serpents that roamed in the Garden of Eden were not poisonous because they simply represented a love of what is sensual. When such love is in its lower rightful place it is not sinful. However, when our love of the physical world becomes dominant and supercedes our love of God and neighbor, it poisons our life and becomes destructive. Hence, when man fell into love of the world, many species of poisonous snakes began to be generated on earth (Fig. 6.6). Scientists who only believe in what they sense outwardly and disregard inner spiritual revelations are like poisonous serpents because they attempt to kill other people's faith in a higher power:

> *In ancient times those were called "serpents" who had more confidence in sensuous things than in revealed ones. But it is still worse at the present day, for now there are persons who not only disbelieve everything they cannot see and feel, but who also confirm themselves in such incredulity by knowledges (scientifica) unknown to the ancients, and thus occasion in themselves a far greater degree of blindness.* (Swedenborg, Emanuel, *Arcana Coelestia* (1749-56), #197, translated by John F. Potts, 1905)

Fig. 6.7. Screech Owl

Most animals live in open air and lighted environments. However, there exist many species that prefer to live in darkness. For example, owls are rarely seen during the daytime. These nocturnal birds have very large eyes and small beaks. They evolved these eyes because they loved darkness more than light. They can now see in darkness but they cannot tolerate the light of the sun. To them, light has become darkness. When humanity fell spiritually, it began to see what is false as true and to believe what is true as false. This is how owls were generated.

> They who have confirmed themselves in faith separated from charity . . . are not in possession of any truths, but merely of falsities. But the falsities of their faith do not indeed appear before them as darkness, that is, as falsities, but they appear to them as if they were lucid, that is, as if they were truths, after they have confirmed themselves in them; but nevertheless, while they are viewed from the light of heaven, which discovers all things, they appear dark; for which reason, when the light of heaven flows into their dens in hell, the darkness is such that they cannot see one another; on which account every hell is closed so as not to leave a crevice open, and then they are in their own light.

> The reason that they do not appear to themselves to be in darkness, but in the light, although they are in falsities, is because their falsities after confirmation appear to them as truths; hence comes their light, but it is the light of infatuation, such as is the light of the confirmation of what is false. This light corresponds to that to which owls and bats owe their sight, to whom darkness is light, and light darkness; yea, to whom the sun itself is thick darkness; eyes like these have they after death, who, during

their abode in the world, confirmed themselves in fal-
sities to such a degree as to see falsity as truth and
truth as falsity. (Swedenborg, Emanuel, *Apocalypse*
Explained (1757-9), #695, translated by John Whitehead, 1911.)

Fig. 6.8. Rats and Bats

Like owls, moles, mice, rats and bats also prefer darkness (Fig. 6.8). Moles are mammals that have adapted to
subterranean life, they have cylindrical bodies, insignificant eyes and ears, and large paws. They can tolerate high
levels of carbon dioxide and need very little oxygen. Rats
love the smells and textures of dark, filthy and unclean environments such as sewers. These mammals were
generated on earth when the human race abused its
freewill and began to love what is useless, evil and selfish.
Such creatures can also be perceived in hell because they
correspond to evil loves:

Influx from hell produces those forms which are evil
forms of use in places where there are corresponding el-
ements. The elements that correspond to evil forms of
use, that is, to malignant herbage and harmful animals,
are those of carrion, putrefaction, excrement and dung,
rot, and urine. In places where these elements exist,
therefore, such herbage and vermin spring up, and in

tropical zones larger creatures of a like character, such as snakes, basilisks, crocodiles, scorpions, mice and rats, and others. (Swedenborg, Emanuel, *Divine Love and Wisdom* (1763) , #341, Translated by N. B. Rogers, 1999)

The bat is a peculiar flying mammal that has adapted to the obscurity of caves. Most bats have very small eyes and poor eyesight but they have very evolved powerful ears by which they are able to navigate in the dark through the use of sonar. Certain bats survive on the blood they suck in the darkness of night from other unsuspecting animals such as cows. Another interesting characteristic of bats is that they like to hang upside down on the ceiling of caves. They are analogous to some human beings who perceive reality upside down. They see what is true as false and what is false as true.

Fig. 6.9. Pack of Wolves Attacking their Prey

Unlike sheep, wolves have a mind and a will of their own. Such creatures have no need for a shepherd because they exclusively rely upon their own self. Although they do like solitude, in order to satisfy their voracious appetites, they tend to gather into packs to hunt and prey on young, weak and innocent animals (Fig. 6.9). If they are attacked, wolves will immediately retaliate with hatred, revenge and lethal violence. When man falls into evil, he begins to misuse his rational faculty to prey on all those who are innocent and helpless through cunning and maliciousness. Such was the inner heart of those false preachers and prophets who were responsible for the appearance of foxes, jackals and wolves on earth:

> There are some who profess holiness, and in this way persuade others, since they appear to be holy, when nevertheless they are "ravening wolves" and are without conscience. By some pretext or another, by artifice and deceit, they crave for their neighbor's goods, and, if possible, provided fear is absent, they carry them off; and they persuade others, including princes and kings, to plunder the goods of others in this manner. They do this without conscience although they profess to act from conscience. (Swedenborg, Emanuel, *Spiritual Experiences* (1765), #1353, translated by J. F. Buss)

Insects are invertebrates that are readily identified by their diminutive size (Fig. 6.10). There are many species of insects but most have a three-part body, three pairs of legs, compound eyes and a pair of antennae. Aside from bees which produce wax and honey and silkworms which provide silk, most insects are considered pests. For example, mosquitoes pierce human skin, suck human blood and spread diseases. Due to Pharaoh's hardness of heart, the Egyptians were also cursed by the plague of flies. When the human mind is enmeshed in the natural level of sensuality, it generates conceptual insects such as worry, fear and doubt.

Fig. 6.10. Various Types of Insects

These flying things, so small and pernicious, are representative in the Word of God of thoughts which fly across the mind of bad persons, and which are continually either leading them into vain conceits, or, into vicious, biting, and destructive ideas concerning others. Our Lord describes these,--at least of the lighter class,--when He exhorts, as you will read in the 6th of Matthew, to lay up treasure in heaven, where neither moth nor rust doth corrupt, and where thieves do not break through nor steal. The moths are vain foppish thoughts, which hit about the soul of a light and frivolous individual, and, eating into all that is solid, are like moths which destroy our garments. (Bayley, Jonathan, From Egypt to Canaan, New Church Press, London, 1869.)

Insects are so small that we are not disturbed by their individual physical appearance. But imagine if these same insects were as large as the human form and they lived among us. They would in fact appear as monsters with thorny limbs, bulging eyes and grotesque faces (Fig. 6.11). An individual insect, by itself, cannot do much damage and it can be eradicated. However, when these creatures gather in large numbers, they can become very destructive. Swarms of locusts have been known to advance like black clouds into farm fields where they cause devastation like armies of soldiers. They also have powerful jaws by which they can devour large amounts of plant life. They correspond to the falsehoods that consume the Truths and Goods of the church in man. In the book of Revelation, which describes the end of the Christian Church, there is a reference to locusts as armies of war:

Fig. 6.11. Face of a Locust

And the likenesses of the locusts were like unto horses prepared for war; and upon their heads as it were crowns like gold, and their faces were as the faces of men. And they had hair as the hair of wom-

en, and their teeth were as those of lions. And they had breastplates, as breastplates of iron; and the voice of their wings was as the voice of chariots of many horses running to war. And they had tails like unto scorpions; and there were stings in their tails: and their power was to hurt men five months. Revelation 9: 7-10

Swedenborg says that these locusts are "the appearances and images of those who have confirmed themselves in faith separated from charity." They believe themselves to be in Truth when, in reality, they are in falsity and evil. Thus, at the end of the age, they will be at war with those who are grounded in the Reality of Love.

The evil within man not only generates disorder in the the plant and animal kingdoms; it also creates conflict, violence, battles and wars in the human kingdom. When a well-known general once said that "war is hell," he was not far from the truth. We do not need to cite the countless wars that have plagued mankind over the ages; but we should know that they all have the same source. All conflict, violence or war is a physical manifestation of the discordant fields of hell. When human beings descend into selfishness and falsehood, they lose touch with the Reality of mutual love, and start to fear, hate and resent those who do not share their selfish loves and false beliefs. Such is the situation in hell because devils only believe in nature and make themselves as gods knowing good and evil. The truth is that there is only One God in the universe. And, when, through self-love, we start to believe that we are our own god, we generate our own hell.

Hence, the levels of hell are filled with many evil spirits or devils who clash with each other by exercising their hatred, fear, cruelty and violence. The rancor, conflict and violence in the conceptual spaces of hell usually manifest on the natural human level as physical hostility, aggression, violence, war, profanation, destruction, theft, rape and murder (Fig. 6.12). And this violence has only increased in recent years as men create more lethal weapons of war, such as guns, explosives and nuclear arms to perpetuate their evil intentions and actions.

Fig. 6. 12. War in the Streets of a City

Just like hateful human armies destroy innocent citizens and insects devastate farm lands, viruses and malignant cells infect our human body and cause disease and death. The aging of the human physical body is a normal and harmonious process. However, the cause of most human diseases must have its origin in the distorted fields of hell. No disease can ever be generated from Heaven because Heaven is the realm of spiritual order from which the human structure evolved. In fact, Heaven must be the source of all spiritual, mental, biological and natural order and healing.

Scientists have recently discovered that most human diseases can be identified in our DNA. The propensity to manifest diseases is past on from one generation to the next through heredity. And, since we enfold within our own being all the evolution of humanity on earth, this would explain why humanity is plagued with so many diseases. Our DNA contains genetic material that is in disorder because humanity fell into the hell of self-love and self-intelligence. Until we reform our mind and regenerate our will, we will continue to manifest diseases that correspond to our mental and spiritual disorder.

Many of us believe that there are still too many cases of horrifying diseases today. However, when the Lord descended on Earth, the situation was even more deplorable. There were then many people who were plagued with grave physical diseases such as blindness, paralysis and leprosy as well as widespread mental illnesses such as schizophrenia. There are many stories in the New Testament where the Lord encounters these distressed human beings and He is able to heal those who have faith in Him.

We have seen that the human biological body is in correspondence with the form of Heaven. Hence, it is the Love and Wisdom from Heaven that inflow into our human body by correspondence and influx that keep our body healthy and alive. When this flow is obstructed in any way, we lose our spiritual and mental protection, and disorder from hell is able to infect our human organization and generate parasites such as viruses as well as unhealthy or cancer cells.

Fig. 6.13. Adenovirus

Viruses are minute foreign organisms that are able to infect our human biological cells and replicate. They consist of genetic material (DNA or RNA) encased in proteins and lipids. The shape of some of these viruses are simple geometric forms that we have already encountered when we studied the beginnings of biological life (Fig. 6.13). However, unlike healthy biological cells whose nucleus is linked to the harmony of Heaven, their own nucleus is a vortex that is in correspondence with the distorted fields of hell. Swedenborg was able to see how evil spirits from hell induce diseases in human beings on earth:

> *All the infernals induce diseases, but with a difference according to the part to which they are attached, so that they may act from the opposite, to wit, in opposition to those in heaven, to whom the parts of the body correspond - for there are opposites to every society in heaven; for, as angels or*

angelic societies preserve in connection and sound-
ness all things in man, so infernals, from the opposite
[side], divide them. But it is only permitted them to
inflow into the cupidities and falsities pertaining to
man - not into man's organs. Only when man falls
into disease, then they inflow also into those
[organs] in man where the disease is; for nothing
ever exists with man, save by a cause from the spiri-
tual world. Man supposes that such things exist in
him, and that there is nothing outside him that acts;
when, yet, every natural has its cause from a spiritu-
al, otherwise it would be without a cause; but, still,
this does not interfere with the fact that they can be,
and also ought to be, cured, or made sound, by natu-
ral means. The Lord's providence then concurs with
such means: and thus, also, man is kept the longer
away from faith concerning a providence in the mi-
nutest particulars; for, if he should believe this, and
afterwards deny it, he would profane a sacred truth,
which is itself a most dreadful hell. (Swedenborg,
Emanuel, *Spiritual Experiences* (1765), #4585, translated by J. F. Buss)

Like Heaven consists of angels and societies of angels,
our human body consists of organic biological cells and organs of cells. In Heaven, every angel or society of angels
also enfolds the knowledge of the whole of Heaven within itself because Heaven is holographic. Similarly, in the
human body, every cell embeds the blueprint of the
whole human body within its DNA. There are also certain
angels and societies of angels in Heaven that are responsi-

ble for preserving Heaven in a state of holiness and de-
fending it from any spiritual infection of evil from hell.
Hence, when we are in conjunction with Heaven, our human physical body is equally protected from physical
infections through correspondence and influx. However,
when we freely and consistently believe the falsehoods
that are flowing into our mind from hell and freely put
their corresponding evil lusts into action, we are disconnected from Heaven and affiliated with the discordant
fields of hell. Hell is then able to penetrate our mind and
heart and, by correspondence, into our physical body. As
a result, our human biological organization loses its protection and healing capacity. We then become prone to
the various diseases that correspond to the diverse evils
and falsities of hell. For example, cancer cells are cells that
no longer hold the information of the human organization
which has its source in Heaven. Cancer spreads to other
parts of the human body because our human body is also
holographic. All human biological cells enfold the information of the whole human body. And, when this
information is compromised, all parts of the human body
are equally affected.

We have seen that Divine Love is realized by means of
Wisdom and Use. All created beings were designed to
wisely realize the purpose of the universe through their
particular function or use. All useful beings cooperate in
realizing the purpose of creation which is ultimately fulfilled in a Heaven of angels from the human race. However, when we freely misuse and abuse our powers of spiritual liberty and rationality, we are linked with a

corresponding hell and we begin to manifest its nefarious, irrational and evil uses and abuses on Earth:

All things that are evil uses are in hell, and all things that are good uses are in heaven. Before it can be seen that all evil uses that take form on earth are not from the Lord but from hell, something must be premised concerning heaven and hell, without a knowledge of which evil uses as well as good may be attributed to the Lord, and it may be believed that they are together from creation; or they may be attributed to nature, and their origin to the sun of nature. From these two errors man cannot be delivered, unless he knows that nothing whatever takes form in the natural world that does not derive its cause and therefore its origin from the spiritual world, and that good is from the Lord, and evil from the devil, that is, from hell. By the spiritual world is meant both heaven and hell. In heaven are to be seen all those things that are good uses. In hell are to be seen all those that are evil uses. These are wild creatures of every kind, as serpents, scorpions, great snakes, crocodiles, tigers, wolves, foxes, swine, owls of different kinds, bats, rats, and mice, frogs, locusts, spiders, and noxious insects of many kinds; also hemlocks and aconites, and all kinds of poisons, both of herbs and of earths; in a word, everything hurtful and deadly to man.

Such things appear in the hells to the life precisely like those on and in the earth. They are said to appear there; yet they are not there as on earth, for they are mere correspondences of lusts that swarm out of their evil loves, and present themselves in such forms before others. Because there are such things in the hells, these abound in foul smells, cadaverous, stercoraceous, urinous, and putrid, wherein the diabolical spirits there take delight, as animals do in rank stenches. From this it can be seen that like things in the natural world did not derive their origin from the Lord, and were not created from the beginning, neither did they spring from nature through her sun, but are from hell. That they are not from nature through her sun is plain, for the spiritual inflows into the natural, and not the reverse. And that they are not from the Lord is plain, because hell is not from Him, therefore nothing in hell corresponding to the evils of its inhabitants is from Him. (Swedenborg, Emanuel, *Divine Love and Wisdom* (1763), #339, translated by John C. Ager, 1890.)

Chapter 7

TRUTH AND FALSEHOOD

We have seen that Truth is the harmonic form of Divine Love. And this Truth is synonymous with the beautiful Heavens of conceptual space. Such was the mind of humanity during its age of innocence. However, when humanity fell into self-love and self-intelligence, man generated distorted emotional fields of energy or hells. Hence, today, man's mind is not only filled with True ideas and thoughts emanating from Heaven; it is equally influenced by distorted ideas, falsities, fantasies and lies proceeding from hell. Presently, man is in spiritual equilibrium where he can choose to believe what is True or what is false.

When the Israelitish Church was consummated, man's mind was so flooded with falsehood and evil that some people's minds were overwhelmed by evil spirits. This was because the Word had descended all the way down to the material level. And, although the Jews possessed the literal Word, they were completely ignorant of its corresponding Spiritual and Celestial Truth. In the New Testament, there is ample evidence to suggest that many people were suffering from grave mental diseases such as schizophrenia, depression and psychosis.

Like our human biological body is a chaotic fractal, our own human mind must also be chaotic and fractal. This also means that the state of our mind can descend all the way down to the level of complete disorder and total confusion. This is usually what happens when we experience a nervous break down or fall into mental depression. Such a catastrophic descent is usually triggered by some tragic event in our life. During such moments, our illusions are shattered and our life on Earth seems to lose all meaning and purpose. Such a state of falsehood also deprives us of all motivation and physical energy because the source of all energy is Divine Love. This personal tumultuous flood of falsehoods is analogous, on a universal scale, to the Biblical floods experienced by humanity at the end of a spiritual age.

In fact, during such periods of confusion and agony, we are experiencing the dark night of the soul. However, as we now know, chaos still embeds the seed of order and we can never lose our essential connection with God. This link is always present through His strange attractor of Love. It is also during these chaotic periods that we are compelled to change our loves and beliefs as well as our whole attitude towards life on Earth. In some ways, a nervous breakdown is a kind of near-death experience on the mental level. Our mind has almost died. And, like a near-death experience, such a mental shock tends to completely transform a person's loves and beliefs. During such anguishing periods, we discover a very profound Truth: by our own self or without God, we are powerless, helpless and stupid. At that point of complete fear and despair, we reach the end of our rope because there is nothing else we can do. And it is often during such darkness in our life that we choose to surrender to Love. In fact, at that crucial moment, we are switching from fear and dependence on our self and into faith in a higher power. This is how the strange attractor of Love is able to lift us up from the pit of spiritual darkness and into higher Light. It is also not a surprising fact that alcoholics, drug and sex addicts must also descend all way down to the bottom of the barrel of their addiction before they decide to change their way of life.

There are many references to *the pit* and *lower earth* in the Bible. According to the Bible's spiritual sense, these words always mean states of conceptual darkness or disorder that are very close to hell. Many of us may also be compelled to remain for a period of time in these dark states after death in order to discard all the false assumptions that we may have accumulated during our life on Earth. We cannot be raised into the True fields of Heaven until our mind is purged of all that is false. While on Earth, Joseph and Jeremiah both spent some time in the pit. But after these difficult experiences, they were raised by the Lord:

*I will extol thee, O Lord; for thou hast lifted me
up, and hast not made my foes to rejoice over me. O
Lord my God, I cried unto thee, and thou hast healed
me. O Lord, thou hast brought up my soul from the
grave: thou hast kept me alive, that I should not go
down to the pit. Sing unto the Lord, O ye saints of
his, and give thanks at the remembrance of his holiness. For his anger endureth but a moment; in his
favour is life: weeping may endure for a night, but joy
cometh in the morning. And in my prosperity I said, I
shall never be moved. Lord, by thy favour thou hast
made my mountain to stand strong: thou didst hide
thy face, and I was troubled. I cried to thee, O Lord;
and unto the Lord I made supplication. What profit is
there in my blood, when I go down to the pit? Shall
the dust praise thee? shall it declare thy truth? Hear,
O Lord, and have mercy upon me: Lord, be thou my
helper. Thou hast turned for me my mourning into
dancing: thou hast put off my sackcloth, and girded
me with gladness; To the end that my glory may sing
praise to thee, and not be silent. O Lord my God, I will
give thanks unto thee for ever.* Psalm 30

Now, the end of the Israelitish Church was analogous
to a complete mental breakdown. The Word had reached
matter or total spiritual darkness. When the Word has fully involved or degenerated, it is ripe and ready to return
into the holy fields of Heaven. Unlike the previous churches, which were restored through the seed of a righteous
and loving human being such as Noah, Abram or Moses,
the state of the human race required a special Divine In-

tervention. God not only needed to reestablish spiritual equilibrium within the contaminated field of human energy; He also required to sow the seeds of Truth in the human mind and generate a coherent Celestial-Spiritual-Natural-Material human body in order to raise the Word back into Heaven.

In the beginning of the New Testament, we are told Jesus was born from a human virgin, Mary. Hence, the ovum from which Jesus was born was human flesh and this egg embedded all the history and sins of humanity that had accumulated at that time. However, we are also informed that this ovum was not impregnated by a human sperm; it was fecundated by the Holy Spirit of God. Thus, we can conclude that Jesus was both human and Divine. He was the "Son of Man" but also the "Son of God." This was necessary because this is how God would be able to reconcile humanity with His Divine Love. After Jesus resisted spiritual temptation from the hells, humiliated and glorified His human flesh, His body became the body by which we could be raised into Heaven.

When the Word reaches the end of matter, it begins to move up again or reflect into Heaven. The Christian Church was the first phase of this ascension. In order to climb into Heaven, we needed the Truth and Jesus was the Truth manifested in the flesh of humanity. His body became the body of God. And His soul continues to be God the Father. This is clearly expressed in the narrative of the New Testament. For example, when Jesus is delivered unto Pilate and he asks Him if He is a king, Jesus answers:

*My kingdom is not of this world: if my kingdom
were of this world, then would my servants fight,
that I should not be delivered to the Jews: but now is
my kingdom not from hence.....Thou sayest that I am
a king. To this end have I been born, and to this end
am I come into the world, that I should bear witness
unto the truth. Every one that is of the truth heareth
my voice.* John 18:36-37

Then Pilate poses the rhetorical question: "What is
Truth?" Due to the fallen state of the human mind and the
disorder in the world, many people today are also convinced that there is no absolute Truth and that Truth is a
matter of opinion. This is the situation in hell because hell
is a realm of conceptual darkness, fantasies, opinions, lies,
confusion and insanity. But in the realm of Reality or
Heaven, there is only One Truth. And all angels are able to
perceive this Truth inwardly and see its beauty manifested
in their projected outer environment by correspondence.
Hence, if Jesus is king and His kingdom is the Kingdom of
Heaven, He must be Truth itself. And Divine Love (Father)
came down as Divine Truth (Son) in the physical world to
sow the seeds of Truth in the collective mind of humanity
and show us the Way that leads to Heaven. This is why Jesus says:

*I am Way, the Truth and the Life, no one comes to
the Father except through me.* John 14:6

When we understand how the universe was generated
from Divine Love in conceptual space, we realize that the

incarnation of Love as the Messiah on Earth was the most significant event in the history of humanity. Through the incarnation and crucifixion of Jesus (YEHOSHUA or YHVH saves), God collapsed the wave-function of Divine Love and entered the history of the world. The collective field of human energy was fertilized with Truth, and Love was fully realized. The body of Jesus then became the means by which we could be raised into Heaven:

For this is the will of my Father, that every one that beholdeth the Son, and believeth on him, should have eternal life; and I will raise him up at the last day. John 6:40

Now, the last day is the day of our physical death. If we behold and believe the Son, we will eventually be raised into the eternal life of Heaven. But how do we see the Son or Truth? In conceptual space, to perceive is to understand with our mind. And since Truth and Love are conjoined, we will only perceive Truth if we live a life of unselfish and innocent Love. When Jesus was in the world, most everyone could see Him physically but very few were able to perceive who He was in conceptual space. In fact, the Scribes and Pharisees thought He was just another finite human being who was blaspheming their abstract idea of God. Their natural and narrow mind was not able to think otherwise.

After Jesus is crucified and resurrected, some of His disciples rush to His tomb. And what they discover is not what they expect. They find the clothes in which He was buried but His body is completely absent. This is an important detail. Here, we uncover that even Jesus' physical body has been completely glorified or spiritualized. And this is later confirmed in the narrative when He mysteriously and miraculously appears to His disciples as they are having supper. He even eats physical food with them to prove this:

> And as they thus spake, Jesus himself stood in the midst of them, and saith unto them, Peace be unto you.
>
> But they were terrified and affrighted, and supposed that they had seen a spirit. And he said unto them, Why are ye troubled? and why do thoughts arise in your hearts? Behold my hands and my feet, that it is I myself: handle me, and see; for a spirit hath not flesh and bones, as ye see me have. And when he had thus spoken, he shewed them his hands and his feet. And while they yet believed not for joy, and wondered, he said unto them, Have ye here any meat? And they gave him a piece of a broiled fish, and of an honeycomb.
>
> And he took it, and did eat before them. And he said unto them, These are the words which I spake unto you, while I was yet with you, that all things must be fulfilled, which were written in the law of Moses, and in the prophets, and in the psalms, concerning me. Luke 24: 36-44

Swedenborg emphasized that we cannot be fully conjoined with an abstract God. However, after God's physical incarnation as Jesus (YEHOSHUA) the Christ (Messiah), we are able to experience a close and personal relationship with God. Even though we may not have been present when He was on Earth, when we read the New Testament, hear the Lord's own words and discover how He lived His life, we can form an affectionate relationship with God. After Jesus' body is glorified, it becomes the Divine-Human body which connects Heaven and earth, God and the Universal Church of humanity.

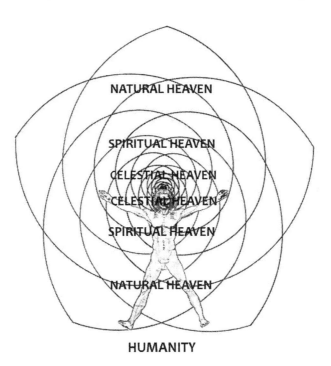

HUMANITY

Fig. 7.1. Heaven as the Divine Human Body of Jesus

These ideas are well-corroborated throughout the New Testament. For example, when Jesus says to Nathaniel that He saw him praying under the fig tree, Nathaniel is amazed by the Lord' s omniscience. Then the Lord adds that he will be even more astonished by what will happen later:

> *Jesus answered and said unto him, Because I said unto thee, I saw thee under the fig tree, believest thou? thou shalt see greater things than these. And he saith unto him, Verily, verily, I say unto you, Here- after ye shall see heaven open, and the angels of God ascending and descending upon the Son of man.* John 1:50-51

The Son of Man is Jesus' body or Divine humanity. It is by descending on this ladder that angels are now able to in- fluence humanity on Earth. And it is equally by way of this Divine Human body that human beings on Earth are able to generate an angelic body of spiritual Light and rise into the harmonic fields of Heaven (Fig. 7.1)

Every word that Jesus speaks in the New Testament is Truth. However, in order to understand or see the beauty of Truth, our mind must be harmonically organized. And, since our understanding flows forth from what we really love, our will must also be harmonic, innocent or un- selfish. Only such a human will can believe and acknowledge Truth. Hence, those human beings who had an innocent heart believed in Jesus while others were re- pelled by the Light of His Truth:

When Jesus spoke again to the people, he said, "I am the light of the world. Whoever follows me will never walk in darkness, but will have the light of life." John 8:12

And this is the judgment, that the light is come into the world, and men loved the darkness rather than the light; for their works were evil. For every one that doeth evil hateth the light, and cometh not to the light, lest his works should be reproved. But he that doeth the truth cometh to the light, that his works may be made manifest, that they have been wrought in God. John 3:19-21

We have seen that Truth is conceptual beauty within our mind, an infinite and complex harmony between conceptual order and chaos. But, after the hells were generated, the spiritual world of our mind split into two. The Kingdom of Heaven was the kingdom God, Light, Harmony and Truth while the so-called kingdom of hell was the kingdom of darkness, disorder, falsehood and selfishness. Hence, as human beings on Earth, we are in spiritual freedom or equilibrium. And we are able to freely choose to believe the Truth that is in-flowing into us from the Light of Heaven or the falsities that rise up from the dark pits of hell.

If we read the words of Jesus in the New Testament, we will discover that what He preaches is in complete agreement with what we have uncovered in the previous chapters of this book. However, we will also notice that the people around Him, the Scribes, Pharisees and even

His disciples often misinterpreted what He was communicating because they had no spiritual comprehension and only understood His words literally. They even erroneously thought that He came down to set up an earthly kingdom and make them rich and powerful. The fact is that Jesus descended to Earth from the conceptual space of Heaven. And, since His desire was to raise us into Heaven, His words were designed to inform us on how to accomplish this task by intending, thinking, speaking and doing what is Good and True.

Jesus made it abundantly clear that the kingdom He was setting up was not a material kingdom. In reality, He was establishing a kingdom of Love and Truth in the conceptual space of our inner mind and heart:

> *And being asked by the Pharisees, when the kingdom of God cometh, he answered them and said, The kingdom of God cometh not with observation: neither shall they say, Lo, here! or, There! for lo, the kingdom of God is within you.* Luke 17:20-21

Now, since Jesus was omniscient, He understood that humanity had descended to a very low state and that the mind of many people was flooded with falsehoods. And, although He had compassion for the masses, He reserved judgment for the Pharisees because they were hypocrites. It was evident that the leaders of the church were exalting themselves above others and filling their minds with more lies:

Jesus said unto them, If God were your Father, ye would love me: for I proceeded forth and came from God; neither came I of myself, but he sent me. Why do ye not understand my speech? even because ye cannot hear my word. Ye are of your father the devil, and the lusts of your father ye will do. He was a murderer from the beginning, and abode not in the truth, because there is no truth in him. When he speaketh a lie, he speaketh of his own: for he is a liar, and the father of it. And because I tell you the truth, ye believe me not. Which of you convinceth me of sin? And if I say the truth, why do ye not believe me? He that is of God heareth God's words: ye therefore hear them not, because ye are not of God. John 8:42-47

Throughout the ages, many misconceptions have arisen with regard to the meaning of "the devil" and "Satan." Fortunately, Swedenborg, by penetrating into the realms of spiritual reality, was able to refute most of these fallacies. Whenever these words appear in the Bible, they always refer to the distorted fields of hell. Swedenborg discovered that, just as Heaven, which consists of angels, is the Divine Human body of God, hell, which consists of a multitude of devils, as an agglomeration, appears as a monstrous being or "devil." And, since Heaven is divided into two main categories or kingdoms, hell must be equally divided. Falsity is in opposition to Truth while evil is in opposition to Good. Those who are mainly in falsehoods are called "satans" while those who are mostly in self-love or evil are named "devils."

Like the cynical Pilate asked "What is Truth?" many people are still under the false impression that there is no absolute Truth. When the human mind descends into the darkness, confusion and disorder of hell, everyone has his own opinions. But we have already derived that Truth must be the harmonic organization or form of Love. Truth must be infinitely rational like the vortical relationship between quaternions. Hence, any idea that is not harmonic or rational is false. Truth is conceptual beauty. In physical space, this harmony is manifested in the harmonic physical form and life of the human body. In conceptual space, this harmony subsists as the harmonic rational form of Heaven. Hence, Jesus' body must be Heaven and the temple of God (Divine Love).

Once again, we have complete confirmation of this in the narrative of Jesus' life and actions. During Jesus' time, the Word had become so corrupted that people were conducting business in the temple of God. They were selling doves, sheep and oxen. And, when Jesus saw this, He drove the traders out of the temple. The Pharisees thought this was very arrogant behavior and asked Him to give them a sign that He had the power and right to do this:

> *Jesus answered and said unto them, Destroy this temple, and in three days I will raise it up. Then said the Jews, Forty and six years was this temple in building, and wilt thou rear it up in three days? But he spake of the temple of his body.* John 2: 19-21

Jesus' body was the real temple of God. But the Pharisees understood everything literally. Truth is Heaven within our mind. And, like there is a physical reality, there is a conceptual reality. If we have no knowledge of this internal or conceptual reality, we will subsist in the conceptual darkness of our opinions, lies and falsehoods. And, presently, the only source from which we can obtain this Truth is the Word:

> But no one can so act until he has been taught, for example, that there is a God, that there is a heaven and a hell, that there is a life after death, that God ought to be loved supremely, and the neighbor as oneself, and that what is taught in the Word, ought to be believed because the Word is Divine. Without a knowledge and acknowledgment of these things man is unable to think spiritually; and if he has no thought about them he does not will them; for what a man does not know he cannot think, and what he does not think he cannot will. So it is when man wills these things that heaven flows into his life, that is, the Lord through heaven, for the Lord flows into the will and through the will into the thought, and through both into the life, and the whole life of man is from these. All this makes clear that spiritual good and truth are learned not from the world but from heaven, and that one can be prepared for heaven only by means of instruction.

> Moreover, so far as the Lord flows into the life of any one He instructs him, for so far He kindles the will with the love of knowing truths and enlightens the

thought to know them; and so far as this is done the interiors of man are opened and heaven is implanted in them; and furthermore, what is Divine and heavenly flows into the honest things pertaining to moral life and into the just things pertaining to civil life in man, and makes them spiritual, since man then does these things from the Divine, which is doing them for the sake of the Divine. For the things honest and just pertaining to moral and civil life which a man does from that source are the essential effects of spiritual life; and the effect derives its all from the effecting cause, since such as the cause is such is the effect. (Swedenborg, Emanuel, *Heaven and Hell (1758)*, #512, translated by John C. Ager, 1900.)

As we can see, we can even live a moral life and not be in the Truth of Heaven. If our moral life is rooted in self-love and self-intelligence, it is only natural and does not connect us with the Truth of Heaven. Even the Pharisees who were performing all the religious rituals and tithing money to the poor were not in Truth. Why? They were doing all this for their own glorification and attributing all the good they were doing to themselves. Hence, they were still in self-love, self-righteousness and self-intelligence and disconnected from Heaven. In fact, as Jesus proclaimed, they were affiliated with the falsehoods and evils of hell.

To believe that only the physical world exists, that our mind is only the result of the organization of the complex neural network of our physical brain or that love is only the outcome of molecules or hormones in our blood is to believe what is false. Divine Love and Truth were already present within God or the Infinite One before the spiritual and physical universe came into existence. We are returning or evolving to Heaven and God because this was God's plan before He generated the universe from His own Substance (Love) and Form (Truth).

Many of us believe what is false because we are deceived by our sensual mind (serpent). We erroneously believe that only the physical world is real because we perceive its forms and touch its substances. We do not believe that God and Heaven exist because we cannot see their forms or touch their substances. However, the reason we cannot see and touch Heaven physically is because Heaven is not a physical realm; it is a conceptual and emotional realm. Heaven is God's conceptual form. And we are able to see or perceive the conceptual forms of Heaven by means of our rational mind and feel its substances by means of our harmonic emotions. Since the emotional and conceptual realm is holographic, after we die physically, we will also be able to perceive and feel these inner ideas and emotions as representative images. Some prophets were even able to experience these spiritual visions while still alive in the physical world.

Many people also contend that, unlike science, which is knowledge that can be ascertained and verified through physical experiment, religion, theology and philosophy are domains of human speculation and belief. And we can never really know what is True. However, when we realize that the scientific laws of the physical world were in fact derived from *the principle of stationary action*, which is the behavior of physical Light, we can conclude that Truth or conceptual Light is even more real than physical Light. This is because physical Light is simply Divine Love in action. And Truth is the form of Love. The Ten Commandments are the laws of Heaven or the conceptual order of our mind. And this order is Divine Truth. The only way to subsist in the conceptual order of Heaven is by acknowledging Truth and practicing Love. Otherwise, our mind will continue to subsist in the confusion and disorder of hell.

It is a fact that all human beings are born in ignorance and innocence. And most of us spend twenty to thirty years of our life on earth educating our self. However, most of the knowledge that we acquire in the world is about the world, its natural science, its geography and history. Some of us may also study mathematics, philosophy, art and literature. And these mental disciplines may begin to cultivate our rational mind. However, the only place we can acquire real knowledge about the Truth of our mind is in the Word of God. The Word is in fact arranged according to the conceptual proportions of Heaven. The stories in the Bible are also organized like a fractal. And every story in the Word is an image of the whole Word. This is probably why the Bible enfolds both history and prophecy. We are not only constrained by the sins of our past but also influenced by the possibilities and providence of the future.

When Jesus restored the sight of a man who was born blind, the disciples asked Him if this man's blindness was the result of the man's sins or of his parents. Jesus answered:

> Neither hath this man sinned, nor his parents: but that the works of God should be made manifest in him. I must work the works of him that sent me, while it is day: the night cometh, when no man can work. As long as I am in the world, I am the light of the world. When he had thus spoken, he spat on the ground, and made clay of the spittle, and he anointed the eyes of the blind man with the clay, And said unto him, Go, wash in the pool of Siloam, He went his way therefore, and washed, and came seeing. John 9:1-7

Natural blindness is in correspondence with spiritual blindness. And we are all born spiritual blind or in ignorance. However, God is able to heal this blindness by enlightening our mind with the Truth of His words. The blind man readily believed in Jesus when he was healed. But the Pharisees remained in the darkness of their lies and falsehoods because they refused to believe Him even though they had witnessed His miracles:

> And Jesus said, For judgment I am come into this world, that they which see not might see; and that they which see might be made blind. And some of the Pharisees which were with him heard these words, and said unto him, Are we blind also? Jesus said unto them, If ye were blind, ye should have no sin: but now ye say, We see; therefore your sin remaineth. John 9:35-41

We can now readily conclude that the dramatic events that unfold on planet Earth are a manifestation of what is occurring in the conceptual spaces of our heart and mind. There is an eternal conflict between Truth and falsehood, Good and evil, Heaven and hell. There is an eternal struggle between those who believe that God and Heaven are real and those who believe that the universe is purely material. Some humans also choose to manifest the rational, useful and meaningful purposes of Heaven, while others tend to express the irrational, useless and nefarious purposes of hell. This conflict tends to spill over into the domain of politics where there is still much tension and disagreement. This should be expected because the Earth is the theater where Divine Love is freely and willingly realized. The earthly level is in correspondence with a realm of spiritual equilibrium. We remain for a while in this realm during our life until we permanently choose between Truth and falsehood.

Great authors, such as Shakespeare, Dante and Milton, were those who were able to skillfully express the conflicts that exist within the human mind and heart. Through prose or poetry, they were able to convey humanity's struggle to discover what is True, Just and Beautiful. They narrate the stories of human beings whose mind is still in doubt and confusion and whose heart is torn between natural desire and spiritual conscience. This is the state of human beings on Earth because in the spiritual equilibrium of Earth, we are still able to change our mind and heart.

Chapter 8

GOOD AND EVIL

In the Golden Age, humanity was in a state of Celestial Innocence. Hence, the Adamic people did not even know what evil meant. This is very similar to the state of very young and innocent children who do not ever suspect that they can do anything wrong. Such infants are also ready and willing to love everyone around them and would never expect that anyone would do them any harm. In such a state, the will of man is harmonized with the Goodness of God's Love because God can only intend what is unselfish. However, after man fell into self-love and self-intelligence, man knew both Good and evil. Therefore, Good must be the result of unselfishness and innocence while evil must be the outcome of selfishness and malice.

If God is omnipotent and God's desire was to generate a Heaven of angels, many people also wonder why God did not immediately create these angels directly from the start. Why did it take billions of years of involution and evolution as well as the elaboration of plants, animals and primates on Earth before these primitive human beings could ultimately generate a spiritual body that would be able to subsist in the eternal fields of Heaven? And the answer is simple. God could have created angels instantly but these angels would have been like robots with no will or spiritual freedom of their own. Real angels must necessarily evolve from the material or earthly level in order to acquire a self that is distinct and separate from God.

In order to be a distinct, unique and separate living organism in the universe, we must not only have a nucleus or vortex that connects us with the fractal attractor (vortex) of Divine Love; we must equally possess a membrane that separates us from others. This can be clearly detected in biological cells. A cell has a nucleus of DNA and RNA as well as a membrane which separates it from its environment. In our own case, physically, this membrane is our human skin. But psychologically, this outer membrane is the natural self of experiences and memories we acquire by evolving from the material level. Swedenborg says that, after we die, these memories become dormant but they continue to serve as a container for our eternal spiritual body:

> Man's natural mind consists of spiritual substances together with natural substances. Thought comes from its spiritual substances, not from its nat-

ural substances. The latter recedes when a man dies, but not the spiritual substances. Consequently, after death, when man becomes a spirit or angel, that same mind remains in a form like that which it had in the world. The natural substances of that mind which, as was said, recede by death, make the cutaneous covering of the spiritual body in which spirits and angels are. By means of such a covering, which is taken from the natural world, their spiritual bodies continue in being, for the natural is the ultimate containant. Hence it is that there is no spirit or angel who was not born a man. (Swedenborg, Emanuel, *Divine Love and Wisdom* (1763), #257, translated by D. & C. Harley)

Hence, angels must evolve as human beings from the natural level to acquire this self that makes them free, distinct and separate from God. Angels may be unselfish but they still possess this self. This is the difference between robots and angels. A robot would be compelled to love God. But angels become angels by FREELY and WILLINGLY choosing to love God as human beings on Earth. On Earth, we are free to reject God and love our own self instead. Now, all this implies that our self is simply a receptacle that is able to receive and reciprocate Divine Love. And any Good that we may perform does not belong to us. It belongs to God alone. In fact, the very definition of evil must be selfishness. When we appropriate Good as our own, we are stealing this Good from God. And, whenever we perform any benevolent action, we attribute merit to ourselves and continue to inflate our hellish ego. In Jesus' time, this was exactly what the Pharisees were doing. They were performing all the sacred rituals and tithing money to the poor but they were equally attributing all the glory to themselves and exalting themselves above others.

The faith of the Pharisees was a hypocritical faith because it was rooted in self-love. This is probably why Jesus preferred to socialize with sinners, prostitutes and tax collectors than with self-righteous priests. Since the Christian Church has presently degraded, this hypocritical faith is also prevalent today. Hence, we regularly witness spiritual ministers preaching Truth, Goodness and Love, while behind the scenes, they are secretly intending and doing what is evil. And when they are caught, they pretend to be repentant. As long as we believe that we are doing any good from our self, we are being deceived. We may be able to fool the whole world but God knows the true intentions of our heart. The only reason the Pharisees rejected Jesus was because they did not want to lose their privileges and their stature in the community.

Now, let us remember how we fell into evil. We were tempted by the serpent or our affection for what is sensual. This means that we started to think that reality is solely the material world and forgot that matter was derived and generated from mental and spiritual realities. Due to such a false world view, we began to believe that our well-being depended on what we could acquire from the material world. This was the beginning of lust, greed and fear. Here, we are able to deduce that evil behavior is always linked to false beliefs.

Swedenborg says that the two main loves in Heaven are Love of God and Love of Neighbor while, in hell, they become love of self and love of the world. However, when we know that the material world is temporal and our self is simply an empty recipient, we realize that existence in our egocentric hell is based on lies, deception and foolishness. The truth is that we are completely dependent upon God because all real substances were derived from Divine Love and real forms from Divine Truth.

Most human beings continue to be fooled by their physical senses because the conceptual world is invisible to their sight. Yet, the truth is that the conceptual world is more real than the material world because it is eternal and permanent. In order to rationalize and justify their selfish intentions and actions, some persons also deny the existence of evil and hell. But how can we ever deny that hell and evil exist when we witness the greedy, cruel, violent, perverse and malicious behavior of some human beings on planet Earth? Can we deny the existence of selfish dictators who enforce their hatred and violence for decades? Can we disregard the behavior of child molesters, rapists, thieves and murderers who willingly infringe upon their neighbor's civil liberty? Can we deny that greedy and wealthy capitalists continue to amass vast amounts of wealth while they witness homeless and hungry children in the streets? Can we deny that hell exists, when we witness the absurdity and destruction of war? There is no way to deny that evil and hell do exist. But the states of hell were not created by God; they were willingly generated by selfish human beings over the ages.

Many people also wonder how an omniscient and benevolent God can see all this injustice without responding in any way. However, God is at peace will all this seeming injustice because He knows that His Justice will be realized in the end. The plane of material earth is where man can exercise his freewill. But physical existence is not an end in itself; it is only a means to an end. And that end or purpose is to generate a conceptual Heaven of angels from the human race. Those who freely, willingly and consistently abuse and misuse their human freewill and rationality on Earth ultimately develop a spiritual body of lusts and falsehoods that can only subsist in the eternal darkness and selfishness of hell. And in such hells, they will be compelled to associate with selfish, lustful, greedy, angry and cruel devils like themselves. The eternal fire of hell is the emotional fire of unfulfilled desires while the gnashing of teeth is the disagreements and arguments of sensual and false thoughts. Hence, evil encloses the seed of its bondage, suffering and damnation.

We have seen that the conceptual spaces of Heaven and hell are within us and, if our mind is in falsehoods, fantasies and lies and our will is in hate, anger, envy, lust and greed, we already are in hell. When our breathing stops, our spiritual body disengages from our material body and we experience a judgment in God's Light. After a period of spiritual expurgation, we are then attracted by the spiritual environments that correspond to our real loves and beliefs. And, if our will is evil or selfish, we will be overwhelmed and repelled by Heaven's Light and we will instead be attracted by an obscure spiritual society in hell that exactly matches our evil passions and falsehoods.

If God is continually restoring order through His Divine attractor of Love, we must also ask ourselves: why do evil and hell continue to subsist in the universe? Although God is continually restoring order from chaos and leading us to Heaven and away from hell through His Divine Providence, He cannot compel us to enter Heaven. We can only enter Heaven freely and willingly. This is because our will is who we really are. And we become who we really are by what we freely intend and do:

> The Lord, moreover, never coerces anyone. For nothing to which one is coerced seems one's own, and what seems not one's own cannot be done from one's love or be appropriated to one as one's own. Man is always led in freedom by the Lord, therefore, and reformed and regenerated in freedom. (Swedenborg, Emanuel, *Divine Providence* (1764), #43, translated by William Frederic Wunsch, 1851.)

Similarly, those who are in hell have freely chosen to be there from their own volition and they delight in their own evil. Therefore, they have no one to blame but themselves for being in hell. This is where they have freely and willingly chosen to be.

God is infinitely merciful and Divine Love and Wisdom are always flowing into our own being from Heaven and attempting to restore the state of our mind and heart. But we always reserve the right to freely reject God and follow our selfish lusts and passions. And, when we do so, we in effect generate our own hell of fantasies, lies, bondage and suffering. As we have already discovered, like Chaos and Order, Freedom and Law are connected. In order to be really free, we must obey the Law. But, when we transgress the Law, we lose our freedom and imprison ourselves in an egocentric hell. This would account for the number of hells. There are many hells because there exists a diversity of human vices.

Since our loves and beliefs are directly linked, when our will is evil, our beliefs are false. Hence, even today, most human beings continue to do evil and call it "good." And, when we love what is selfish, we are compelled to rationalize and justify our own evil intentions and actions by means of falsehoods and lies. The fall of man precipitated the human race into negative or hellish states of selfishness, greed, lust, fear and hatred.

As long as we are in the spiritual equilibrium of earth, we can still change our mind and heart. However, when we consistently intend what is not Good and do what is evil, we generate a distorted spiritual body that only has the capacity to reside in the obscure realms of hell. Since the universe is essentially holographic and every being is a wave-function of standing waves that embeds the whole within itself, when our will is in evil and our mind is in falsehood and insanity, we have hell within us. Swedenborg discovered that existence in hell consists mainly of selfish loves and fantasies. In these obscure environments, devils can believe and imagine whatever they desire. And, since these fantasies are not rooted in any substantial reality, they eventually find themselves in the deserted, cruel, filthy, obscure and harsh places that correspond to their state of being. The whole universe is ruled by the One True God of the universe but hell is a realm of fantasy where every devil desires to enforce his own rules through deception, magical arts, threats, fear and punishment:

> When man enters the other life he is received first by angels, who perform for him all good offices, and talk with him about the Lord, heaven, and the angelic life, and instruct him in things that are true and good. But if the man, now a spirit, be one who knew about these things in the world, but in heart denied or despised them, after some conversation he desires and seeks to get away from these angels. As soon as the angels perceive this they leave him. After some interaction with others he at length unites himself with those who are in evil like his own. When this takes place he turns himself away from the Lord and turns his face towards the hell to which he had been joined in the world, in which those abide who are in a like love of evil.
>
> All this makes clear that the Lord draws every spirit to Himself by means of angels and by means of influx from heaven; but those spirits that are in evil completely resist, and as it were tear themselves away from the Lord, and are drawn by their own evil, thus by hell, as if by a rope. And as they are so drawn, and by reason of their love of evil are eager to follow, it is evident that they themselves cast themselves into hell by their own free choice. Men in the world because of their idea of hell are unable to believe that this is so. In fact, in the other life before the eyes of those who are outside of hell it does not so appear; but only so to those who cast themselves into hell, for such enter of their own accord.

Those who enter from a burning love of evil appear to be cast headlong, with the head downwards and the feet upwards. It is because of this appearance that they seem to be cast into hell by Divine power. From all this it can be seen that the Lord casts no one into hell, but everyone casts himself into hell, both while he is living in the world and also after death when he comes among spirits. (Swedenborg, Emanuel, *Heaven and Hell* (1758), #548, translated by John C. Ager, 1900.)

I have seen and been instructed as to the state of the hells in general. Phantasies are what rule there, and they appear real to the life, because those who are there are in phantasies, and have no other life than that of phantasies; if they had not that, they would have none at all, wherefore their phantasies are to them as living realities, perceived with all fullness of sense, as I have learned by multiplied experience, and from having often times conversed with spirits on the subject. They said they knew they were phantasies, to which it was replied that such was the fact, but still they perceived them with perfect sensation, and even with pain and torture; and although they themselves are mere phantasies, yet they cannot otherwise live, as the sum total of their existence is phantasy, inasmuch as they are not in goodness and the truth of faith; for good spirits and angels never perceive such things, inasmuch as they are in truth. (Swedenborg, Emanuel, *Spiritual Experiences* (1765), #4380, translated by J. F. Buss)

I have also been permitted to look into the hells and to see what they are within; for when the Lord pleases, the sight of a spirit or angel from above may penetrate into the lowest depths beneath and explore their character, notwithstanding the coverings. In this way I have been permitted to look into them. Some of the hells appeared to the view like caverns and passages in the rocks extending inward and then downward into an abyss, either obliquely or vertically. Some of the hells appeared to the view like the dens and caves of wild beasts in forests; some like the hollow caverns and passages that are seen in mines, with tunnels extending towards the lower regions. Most of the hells are threefold, the upper one appearing within to be in dense darkness, because inhabited by those who are in the falsities of evil; while the lower ones appear fiery, because inhabited by those who are in evils themselves, dense darkness corresponding to the falsities of evil, and fire to evils themselves. For those who have acted interiorly from evil are in the deeper hells, and those who have acted exteriorly from evil, that is, from the falsities of evil, are in the hells that are less deep.

Some hells present an appearance like the ruins of houses and cities after conflagrations, in which infernal spirits dwell and hide themselves. In the milder hells there is an appearance of rude huts, in some cases contiguous in the form of a city with lanes and streets, and within the houses are infernal spirits engaged in unceasing quarrels, enmities, fightings, and brutalities; while in the streets and lanes, robberies and depredations are committed. In some of the hells there are nothing but brothels, disgusting to the sight and filled with every kind of filth and excrement. Again, there are dark forests, in which infernal spirits roam like wild beasts

*and where, too, there are underground tunnels into
which those flee who are pursued by others. There are
also deserts, where all is barren and sandy, and where in
some places there are ragged rocks in which there are
caverns, and in some places huts. Into these desert
places, are cast out from the hells those who have suf-
fered every extremity of punishment, especially those
who in the world have been more cunning than others
in undertaking and contriving intrigues and deceits.
Such a life is their final lot.* (Swedenborg, Emanuel,
Heaven and Hell (1768), #586, translated by D. Harley,
1958.)

In the moral realm, a lack of balance produces an evil
will. In table 8.1, we can readily see the qualities of a harmonic human will and its excesses and lacks. To be courageous is to will and do what is Good and useful in a way
that is wise. But to act without forethought is to be rash
and to lack the courage to act is to be a coward. To express God's Love, mercy and abundance wisely is to be
generous. But to withhold this Love is to be miserly and to
be extravagant is to be wasteful. To mindfully speak the
Truth is to be honest. But to share information indiscriminately is gossip and to selfishly withhold the Truth from
others is to be secretive. To act wisely is to be in control of
our self. But to react impulsively is to be an automaton
and to over-think and doubt our self is to be indecisive. To
know that our self is only a recipient of God's Love and
Wisdom is to be modest. But to believe that these Goods
and Truths belong to us is to be arrogant and to belittle
and demean our self is stupid. To know that all humans

are our brothers and sisters is to be friendly. But to flatter and be kind to others indiscriminately is to be hypocritical and to argue with those who do not share our values is to be quarrelsome. To desire to do God's will is to be vigorous. But to lack any desire is to be apathetic and to be overly ambitious is to be greedy.

INVOLUTION	HARMONY	EVOLUTION
Rashness	Courage	Cowardice
Extravagance	Generosity	Miserliness
Loquacity	Honesty	Secrecy
Impulsiveness	Self-Control	Indecisiveness
Pride	Modesty	Self-abnegation
Flattery	Friendliness	Quarrelsomeness
Greed	Vigor	Apathy

Table 8.1. Harmonic Proportions of Human Will

In order to enter Heaven, we require a harmonic will. The Lord came into the world to show us the Way to Heaven. His life on Earth was a manifestation of Goodness. To all appearances, the Pharisees also seemed like they were righteous, responsible, religious and God-fearing people. In fact, they performed all the religious rituals meticulously and were well-respected by the community. And yet, Jesus identified them as hypocritical and evil. This is because our actions proceed from our will. And if our will is corrupt and selfish, all our actions are equally evil, no matter how good they may appear to the world. In order to really understand the difference between good and evil, we must turn to the Sermon on the Mount in the New Testament. It is important to notice that Jesus is communicating this spiritual knowledge to His disciples only and not to the masses. This is because, at that time, the state of the human mind was not ready to absorb Jesus' higher teachings. Even the disciples often had difficulty accepting what Jesus was saying:

> *Many therefore of his disciples, when they had heard this, said, This is an hard saying; who can hear it?* John 6:70

After 2000 years of spiritual evolution, the state of our mind has matured and it now becomes possible to really understand what Jesus was communicating to His disciples. It is interesting to note that these sayings are known as the *Beatitudes*. And the word "Beatitude" means real joy or happiness. When our life is driven by self-love and love of the world, our existence is meaningless and purposeless and even our joy is not real; it is a superficial or false joy. Today, many preachers use these teachings in their sermons. However, here, we are going to interpret these *Beatitudes* in the Light of the real knowledge that we have uncovered in this book.

When we choose to live in accordance with the *Beatitudes*, we are embarking upon a completely different kind of life. Our life may not appear to be glamorous, extravagant and lavish as the life we previously lived in the world. However, it will no longer be false; it will be real and blessed by God who is Reality itself. We must remember that we do not just exist in the world; we also subsist in the reality of our mind and heart. And real joy cannot be the outcome of pleasant circumstances in the world; it can only be the result of our harmonious relationship with others and God in the Reality our own heart and mind. To experience the real joy of Heaven, our mind and heart must be in Heaven.

1.Blessed are the poor in spirit: for theirs is the kingdom of heaven.

In order to solve a problem, we must first acknowledge that it exists. However, when our mind is in conceptual darkness, we are blind to our state of being. We erroneously believe that we can see or understand. In such a state of denial, we are like owls which can only see in the dark. In such a state, we see falsehood as Truth and Truth as falsehood, evil as Good and Good as evil. This is like the state of many scientists who are proud of their scientific knowledge and totally reject the revelations of the Bible. When we repudiate all revealed Truth and only believe our physical senses, we remain spiritually blind.

In order to begin to see what is True and hear what is Good, we must acknowledge that we are spiritually blind and that our natural self is evil. In fact, the very definition of evil is selfishness. To realize that we are in evil, that the knowledge that we possess is insignificant and useless, and that we are completely ignorant is to be poor in spirit. It is only when we are in this state that we can perhaps receive some real knowledge or Wisdom from Heaven.

   2.   *Blessed are they that mourn: for they shall be comforted.*

Are we to relinquish our life of worldly pleasures in order to mourn? What kind of blessedness is that! However, when we realize that all these carnal delights do not ever result in any lasting joy and only lead to more intense desires, we understand what this means. After we fell into self-love and love of the world, we lost all real Life, Truth and Love. We then began to live a life that was dead. When we realize that a life of self-glory, worldly pursuits and carnal pleasures is really death, we can mourn for the Life we have lost. An we can then be comforted by the Love and Wisdom of God within us.

   3.   *Blessed are the meek: for they shall inherit the earth.*

When we look around us, we conclude that it is those who have accumulated the most wealth, power and stature in the world that have inherited the earth. But is this the reality? What have they inherited in reality? Nothing! After they die, they will return into the spiritual world with an empty heart and a corrupted mind. In the spiritual world, all the wealth and power of the world is worth nothing. However, when we generate Love within us through a life of loving and useful actions in the world, we inherit all that the Earth is able to give us. Spiritually, the Earth corresponds to the Church. And it is those who are meek that will inherit a New Heaven and a New Earth (Church).

   4.   *Blessed are they which do hunger and thirst after righteousness: for they shall be filled.*

God created the universe in order to generate a Heaven of angels from the human race where He would bestow His gifts upon His creatures. The Lord, when He was on Earth even said:

   And seek not ye what ye shall eat, or what ye shall drink, neither be ye of doubtful mind. For all these things do the nations of the world seek after: and your Father knoweth that ye have need of these things. But rather seek ye the kingdom of God; and all these things shall be added unto you. Fear not, little flock; for it is your Father's good pleasure to give you the kingdom. Luke 12: 29-32

When we realize that our thirst for Truth and hunger for Love is much more important than our thirst for water and our hunger for food, we will begin to concentrate on seeking righteousness. And this righteousness, will ultimately manifest as peace in our mind and pleasant circumstances in our physical life by means of correspondence and influx.

5.   Blessed are the merciful: for they shall obtain
mercy.

We have seen that the Earth or material level of the
universe is essentially a mirror where the Love and Wisdom of God can be freely received and reflected. And in
order to continue to receive God's mercy, we must keep it
flowing through reflection. The Golden Rule is "do unto
others as you would have them do unto you" because the
universe is a fractal that is feeding back upon itself. Our
merciful intentions and actions collapse the wave-function of our being into the vortex of Love where they are
reflected. This is how we continue to obtain mercy from
God.

6.   Blessed are the pure in heart: for they shall
see God.

We see the natural world through our natural eyes. But
we have determined that God is in the conceptual space
of Heaven. Hence, to perceive God, we need conceptual
eyes. In order to begin to see into Heaven, we need to develop and cultivate our rational mind because Heaven is
organized according to the harmonic and infinitely rational proportions of Truth. And, since a true mind can only
be derived from an innocent will, we will only perceive
God if our heart is unselfish, pure and innocent. In fact, infants can see God because they are in innocence. And we
will only enter Heaven when our heart has returned to innocence through Wisdom:

And Jesus called a little child unto him, and set him in the midst of them, And said, Verily I say unto you, Except ye be converted, and become as little children, ye shall not enter into the kingdom of heaven. Whosoever therefore shall humble himself as this little child, the same is greatest in the kingdom of heaven.

Take heed that ye despise not one of these little ones; for I say unto you, That in heaven their angels do always behold the face of my Father which is in heaven. Matthew 18: 2, 3, 10

7. *Blessed are the peacemakers: for they shall be called the children of God.*

When we are still in self-love and love of the world, we perceive the universe upside down. We see Truth as falsehood and Good as evil. Hence, we falsely believe that conflicts, acts of violence and wars are interesting and exciting while we characterize states of Peace as stagnant and boring. But this is completely false. The states of hell are states of conflict, confusion, hatred and cruelty that are meaningless, purposeless and useless because they always culminate in addiction, slavery and suffering. In contrast, the state of Heaven is a state of Peace that is infinitely vibrant, dynamic, creative and alive. Heaven is filled with countless angels and societies of angels. And the form of each of these angels is a unique and different reflection of Truth, their energy or substance is a particular affection of Love and their function is a unique expression of God's Power. But Heaven is in a state of Peaceful activity and creativity because all these angels are harmonically interconnected by Divine Love, Wisdom and Use. Their life is purposeful, meaningful and useful. And they continue to derive more real joy as they proceed to understand more Truth, intend more Good and do what is more useful. This joy and peace increases eternally because Divine Love is infinite. Angels can continue to approach God eternally but they can never reach Him. To be a child of God is to believe in God's Truth, to intend and do His Love and to express His Peace:

Peace I leave with you, my peace I give unto you: not as the world giveth, give I unto you. Let not your heart be troubled, neither let it be afraid. John 14: 27

8. *Blessed are they which are persecuted for righteousness' sake: for theirs is the kingdom of heaven.* Matthew 5: 3-10

When we embark on a life of righteousness, those who are still in love of self and love of the world will naturally be offended by our speech and behavior. Hence, we may be persecuted in the world. We only have to notice how Jesus was mistreated to understand what this means. Human beings tend to malign, marginalize and persecute whatever they do not understand and believe. And, when their will is evil, they justify their evil actions by means of falsehoods and lies. In order to remain in such a state, they must regularly persecute Truth and mock the Word of God or Bible. Thus, many disciples, ministers and prophets were and continue to be persecuted in the world. However, when our mind is in Truth and our will is in Love, our physical body may be attacked but our spiritual body is safe and well-protected. This persecution in the world is also analogous to the conflict that unfolds in the conceptual space of our mind between our natural passions and spiritual conscience. These spiritual battles or temptations are the means by which we can be regenerated and saved.

In the beginning of this book, we claimed that the universe is a dramatic work of art. The artist or writer of this dramatic play is God and its script is the Word of God. But God has bestowed upon every human being the gift of His own substance, Love or freewill. The Earth is the theater where the dramatic story of creation, redemption and salvation unfolds. It is the stage where the eternal battle between Good and evil is manifested. And every human being is an actor playing his part in this eternal play. Every person is free to reciprocate Love or to misuse and abuse it. We can freely choose to cooperate with God and play our part to realize Justice, Goodness and Truth in our own unique and individual way or, instead, we can freely opt to oppose God and play the villain who expresses selfishness, evil and cruelty in the world. But when we die physically, our performance is over and we return into the spiritual world where we are compelled to remove our mask and others can see the real nature of our being. In the spiritual world, there is no hypocrisy and our spiritual body and environment are an exact representation of our real loves and beliefs. In spiritual reality, we are able to clearly see the beauty of Truth and Goodness, and to recognize the ugliness of falsehood and evil.

III
PROPHECY

Chapter 9

A NEW HEAVEN
AND
A NEW EARTH

We have seen that the Word of God not only embeds the history of humanity but its prophecy as well. In the New Testament itself, the Lord prophesies the degradation and eventual end of the Christian Church which He personally raised. But He also foretells that, after these tribulations, the Son of Man will return riding a white horse in the clouds of Heaven. This mysterious prophecy has sparked much confusion in the Christian community. And many preachers who have interpreted the Word literally have mistakenly predicted that there will occur a great physical catastrophe, the world as we know it will end and the Lord will come again in a physical human body, on a physical white horse and in the physical clouds. However, we have already discovered that the Word contains a spiritual sense and the literal stories refer to spiritual or conceptual realities.

Fig. 9.1. A Heaven of Angels from the Human Race

According to the spiritual sense of the Word, the Lord is gradually establishing a conceptual Kingdom in which He can be conjoined with free and loving human beings or angels by Love, Wisdom and Use. The substance of this kingdom is not physical energy; it is spiritual or emotional energy. And the form of this Kingdom is not a physical form; it is a conceptual form or Divine Idea. We have seen in previous chapters of this book that the organization of Divine or Heavenly Love is synonymous with the vortical relationship between quaternions, octonions, sedenions and other hypernumbers. And this harmonic relationship is analogous to the harmonic and fractal relationship between all the parts of the human body. Thus, the form of this Kingdom will consist of an outer Natural Heaven of Natural angels, an inner Spiritual Heaven of Spiritual angels and an inmost Celestial Heaven of Celestial angels (Fig. 9.1).

The Natural angels who are predominantly in Use are in the digestive system of Heaven. They process all the human souls that enter the spiritual world from the human race by separating what is Good from what is evil and what is True from what is false. Those human souls that mainly consist of Good (unselfish) loves and True (rational) beliefs are incorporated into the Heavenly fields while those souls that are mostly in evil (selfish) loves and false beliefs are evacuated out of Heaven and into the discordant fields of hell, just as the nutritious elements of food are digested in the human organism and what is unwholesome is discarded by the colon.

Spiritual angels subsist in the circulatory and pulmonary system or the heart and lungs of Heaven. Since they are essentially in Truth, they make sure that all the societies of Heaven are continually provided and purified with Truth. Like the blood cells in our own human body dispense oxygen and nutrients to every organ in our human body, these angels transfer Truth to every community in Heaven. Truth maintains the organization and order of all things in creation.

Finally, the Celestial angels are located in the inmost center where they receive Celestial Love and Wisdom directly from the Lord. And, since the realization of Divine Love is the whole purpose of the universe, these angels are engaged in the purposes of Heaven. The Celestial level is the brain or nervous system of the universe that assigns a purpose to every being in creation. Thus, the Celestial angels flow into the will of every created being and urge it to realize unselfish or innocent Love.

Since every soul that enters this conceptual Kingdom has evolved from the material realm, it is a wave-function (vortex) of standing waves of emotional energy contained within a natural self of memories. And, even though this Kingdom consists of emotional energies and their conceptual forms or ideas, every being is able to perceive a holographic image or representation of these conceptual forms. Swedenborg refers to these holographic images as *representatives*. These *representatives* are real because they correspond to real emotional energies.

Hence, when we disengage from our material body, we will enter a mental and emotional atmosphere that corresponds exactly to the quality of our own mental and emotional energy. In addition, we will perceive the holographic forms or images that correspond to these energies. Unlike on Earth, where our outer world does not necessarily have to match our inner state of being, in the spiritual world, our holographic environment always matches our emotions and thoughts or our loves and beliefs. This all occurs in accordance with scientific laws.

Heaven is organized according to Truth or conceptual beauty. Hence, if we have the capacity to enter Heaven, we should expect to perceive a realm of beauty and grace. Some of the forms that we will perceive will be familiar but the beauty and variety of the forms that we will encounter will be endlessly diverse and exquisitely proportioned. And the quality of the world that we will experience will be in exact correspondence with the quality of our own loves and beliefs. The more our understanding is wise and the more our will is innocent the more graceful, pleasant and joyful our environment will appear to be:

As all things that correspond to interiors also represent them they are called representatives; and as they differ in each case in accordance with the state of the interiors they are called appearances. Nevertheless, the things that appear before the eyes of angels in heaven and are perceived by their senses appear to their eyes and senses as fully living as things on earth appear to man, and even much more clearly, distinctly and perceptibly. Appearances from this source in heaven are called real appearances, because they have real existence. There are appearances also that are not real, which are things that become visible, but do not correspond to interiors.

To show what the things are that appear to the angels in accordance with correspondences, I will here mention one only for the sake of illustration. By those who are intelligent, gardens and parks full of trees and flowers of every kind are seen. The trees are planted in a most beautiful order, combined to form arbors with arched approaches and encircling walks, all more beautiful than words can describe. There the intelligent walk, and gather flowers and weave garlands with which they adorn little children. Moreover, there are kinds of trees and flowers there that are never seen and cannot exist on earth. The trees bear fruit that are in accordance with the good of love, in which the intelligent are. These things are seen by them because a garden or park and fruit trees and flowers correspond to intelligence and wisdom. That there are such things in heaven is known also on the earth, but only to those who are in good, and who have not extinguished in themselves the light of heaven by means of natural light and its fallacies; for when such think about heaven they think and say that there are such things there as ear hath not heard and eye hath not seen.

Since angels are men, and live among themselves as men do on the earth, they have garments and dwellings and other such things, with the difference, however, that as they are in a more perfect state all things with them are in greater perfection. For as angelic wisdom surpasses human wisdom to such a degree as to be called ineffable, so is it with all things that are perceived and seen by angels, inasmuch as *all things perceived and seen by them correspond to their wisdom.* (Swedenborg, Emanuel, *Heaven and Hell* (1758), #175-177, translated by John C. Ager, 1900.)

This is what the Lord meant when He said:

In my Father's house are many mansions: if it were not so, I would have told you. I go to prepare a place for you. And if I go and prepare a place for you, I will come again, and receive you unto myself; that where I am, there ye may be also. John 14:2-3

After Jesus' crucifixion, glorification, resurrection and ascension, His body became the Divine-Human body of Heaven. God is preparing a place for us in one of the countless societies of Heaven. This place or state will be in exact correspondence with our true loves, beliefs and powers. And our eternal joy in Heaven will be derived from the function we will perform in one of these Heavenly societies.

Although the Lord definitely said that He will come again, He did not mean that He will come in the flesh. There is no need for such a physical incarnation because that Divine Operation has already been fully accomplished 2000 years ago. When He manifested as the Messiah (Christ) on Earth, God completely fulfilled the Scriptures and generated a glorified Celestial-Spiritual-Natural-Material body by which He could raise us into Heaven. He said that this time He will come again riding a white horse in the clouds of Heaven. What does this really mean? Remember that Jesus is the Word of God. And we now know that a white horse corresponds to an understanding of the Word. Clouds both hide and convey the light of the sun like the literal sense of the Word embeds and conceals its spiritual Light or Divine Truth. Thus, translated, this means that God will come again into our heart and mind through a spiritual understanding of the Word or Bible. This is how this New Church or *New Jerusalem* will begin to be established.

A New Heaven and a New Earth really means a new conceptual order in the Heavens of our mind and heart and a New Church on the earth because these two are always linked by correspondence. Swedenborg says that there cannot be a Church or religion without Heaven because this is where the principles and doctrines of the Church originate. These True principles, ideas and doctrines descend from Heaven into the heart and mind of a righteous human being or prophet and they are eventually revealed to the world. There cannot also be a Heaven without a Church because the higher-dimensional levels of Heaven must terminate in the hearts and minds of loving and righteous human beings. Without this physical foundation, Heaven becomes unstable, meaningless and useless. Swedenborg refers to this assembly of faithful and loving human beings as the Universal Church. Like Heaven, this human assembly is as complex, varied, harmonious and coherent as the trillions of cells, organs, glands and members of the human structure:

> *The Lord has provided that there should be some*
> *religion almost everywhere and that everyone who*

believes in God and does not do evil because it is against God should have a place in heaven. Heaven, seen in its entirety, looks like a single individual, whose life or soul is the Lord. In that heavenly person there are all the components that there are in a physical person, differing the way heavenly things differ from earthly ones.

We know that there are within us not only the parts formed as organs from blood vessels and nerve fibers--the forms we call our viscera. There are also skin, membranes, tendons, cartilage, bones, nails, and teeth. They are less intensely alive than the organic forms, which they serve as ligaments, coverings, and supports. If there are to be all these elements in that heavenly person who is heaven, it cannot be made up of the people of one religion only. It needs people from many religions; so all the people who make these two universal principles of the church central to their own lives have a place in that heavenly person, that is, in heaven. They enjoy the happiness that suits their own nature. (Swedenborg, Emanuel, *Divine Providence* (1764), #326, translated by G. F. Dole, 2003)

Now, from history, we know that every Church eventually decays and dies and, when chaos in the world reaches its maximum, the attractor of Love is activated and a new world order begins. However, the Bible foretells that the *New Jerusalem* will be the final Church on the Earth because the Word will be completely raised back into Heaven through the body of Jesus. This is clearly stated in the book of Isaiah the prophet. Instead of degrading, the *New Jerusalem* will continue to improve infinitely:

> *For unto us a child is born, unto us a son is given: and the government shall be upon his shoulder: and his name shall be called Wonderful, Counsellor, The mighty God, The everlasting Father, The Prince of Peace. Of the increase of his government and peace there shall be no end, upon the throne of David, and upon his kingdom, to order it, and to establish it with judgment and with justice from henceforth even for ever. The zeal of the Lord of hosts will perform this.* Isaiah 9:6-7

The book of Revelation contains information regarding this New Church or "New Jerusalem" that is presently beginning to develop within the conceptual spaces of our mind and heart. These conceptual spaces, which consist of emotional energy organized according to rational forms, are even more real than the physical spaces in which we presently exist. In fact, the visions of the prophets are the representatives they perceive in the conceptual spaces of their mind. Hence, what they see always corresponds to spiritual realities. Swedenborg also discovered that all words in the Bible have a consistent meaning throughout its many books because they were all written according to the *science of correspondences*.

The prophet John is exiled to the island of Patmos and is there uplifted by the Lord into the Celestial level of Heaven where he is able to perceive the form of the future. Some people believe that this John was the same John who wrote the Gospel of John and was Jesus' beloved disciple:

And a great sign was seen in heaven; a woman clothed with the sun, and the moon under her feet, and upon her head a crown of twelve stars.

And being with child, she cried, travailing and pained to bring forth. And another sign was seen in heaven; and behold, a great red dragon, having seven heads, and ten horns, and upon his heads seven diadems. And his tail drew the third part of the stars of heaven, and cast them to the earth; and the dragon stood before the woman who was about to *bring forth, that after she had brought forth, he might devour her offspring.*

And she brought forth a son, a male, who was to tend all nations with a rod of iron; and her offspring was caught up unto God and His throne. And the woman fled into the wilderness, where she hath a place prepared by God, that they may nourish her there a thousand two hundred and sixty days. And there was war in heaven, Michael and his angels fought with the dragon, and the dragon fought and his angels. And they prevailed not, and their place was not found any more in heaven. And that great dragon was cast out, that old serpent called the Devil and Satan, that seduceth the whole world; he was cast out into the earth, and his angels were cast out with him. Revelation 12:1-9

The *New Jerusalem* will manifest as a new spiritual order or Heaven within the conceptual spaces of our mind and a New Church on the earth. This New Church is the lamb's wife or bride because the Lord is the bridegroom. She is clothed with the sun because the Lord's Love appears as a spiritual sun in the spiritual world. The moon is under her feet like the reflected Light of faith in Scripture supports the Church. The twelve stars represent all the Heavenly knowledge of Truth that crowns the members of this New Church. The child she is bringing forth represents the New Jerusalem's spiritual doctrines. We have seen that a new order begins as a seed of Truth that emerges from chaos and eventually develops and grows.

The birth of these Heavenly doctrines will be as difficult as a woman's pregnancy and childbirth.

The red dragon represents what remains of the previous church. After 2000 years, the Christian Church has become so corrupted, degraded and deformed that it now resembles a monstrous creature in conceptual space. The leaders of this church have endorsed faith without love, split God into three persons and appropriated God's power and glory to themselves. The seven heads represent "the insanity from the truths of the Word falsified and profaned." Precious stones correspond to the literal sense of the Word. But, when these truths are falsified, they become like diadems on a monstrous dragon.

We have seen that horns correspond to power. When men utilize religion for their own selfish ends, they steal God's power and only produce division, confusion and destruction like a fire-breathing dragon. Hence, sensing that they are about to lose their power, the members of this degraded church will oppose and refute the knowledges of the New Church. They will even attempt to devour or destroy its doctrines. But God will defend and nourish this New Church until it is fully grown. And the angels of Heaven will continue to fight the forces of hell until they are completely subdued and vanquished.

Swedenborg says that the names of archangels in the Bible, such as *Michael* and *Gabriel*, are the names of whole societies of individual angels in Heaven. Therefore, here, we may assume that whole societies of angels will fight swarms of devils in hell until the leaders of the old church are no longer able to exercise any influence and power in the conceptual spaces of our mind. And the devils of hell that were threatening to disrupt spiritual order will be cast out of Heaven and into the world of spirits.

If conceptual space is even more real than physical space, it should not therefore surprise us to learn that the *New Jerusalem* has substance, dimensions and form. In physical space, the dimensions of length, width and height are physical, while in conceptual space they must be conceptual. In Revelation, the *New Jerusalem* or beautiful City of God is described as follows:

> *I saw a new heaven and a new earth, and the first heaven and the first earth had passed away. And I saw the holy city Jerusalem coming down from God out of heaven. The city was foursquare, its length as great as its breadth; and an angel measured the city with a reed, twelve thousand furlongs; the length, the breadth, and the height of it are equal. And he measured the wall thereof, an hundred and forty-four cubits, the measure of a man, that is, of an angel. The building of the wall was of jasper; but the city itself was pure gold, and like unto pure glass; and the foundations of the wall were adorned with every precious stone. The twelve gates were twelve pearls; and the street of the city was pure gold, as it were transparent glass.* Revelation 21: 1, 2, 16-19, 21.

The City of God is a city in our heart and mind. Therefore, it consists of emotional energy and this energy is organized according to a conceptual form or idea. In the conceptual Heavens of our mind, "length means a state of good, breadth a state of truth, and height the distinction between them in accordance with degrees." This city is square because a square represents Justice or righteous-ness in all four corners.

It will be exactly twelve thousand furlongs (12 x 1000). In chapter 1, we saw that numbers refer to order in con-ceptual space. Therefore, numbers in the Bible also have spiritual significance. Twelve times one thousand is the quality of *twelve* refined to a very high degree. In mathe-matics, twelve is the smallest composite number with six divisors (1, 2, 3, 4, 6, 12). In nature, there are twelve months or lunar cycles in a solar cycle or year and the earth travels through twelve constellations in the sky or the twelve signs of the Zodiac. The human brain also has exactly twelve cranial nerves that relay information to the parts of the human body. The number *twelve* is also prevalent throughout the Bible. For example, Jacob had 12 sons. There were 12 tribes of Israel, 12 precious stones in the breastplate of the high priest and Jesus had 12 disci-ples. Finally, the woman clothed with the sun or the Lord'-s New Church has a crown of 12 stars upon her head. This is because *twelve* represents all the Truths and Goods of the Church and Heaven from three degrees and four di-rections (3x4).

In olden days, cities were surrounded by high walls to protect their citizens. In a similar way, the literal sense of the Word always protects its inner Spiritual and Celestial content. You may have noticed how certain people are of-fended and repulsed by the bizarre stories of the literal Bible. This is not an accident. The Bible was purposefully

designed in this way so that only those who really and sin-
cerely desire to know and understand the Truth are able
to move past these high walls and penetrate into the city
or doctrine. Those who are kept out of the *New Jerusalem*
are only prevented to enter by their own lack of desire to
know and understand the Truth. When our heart is in evil
or selfishness, we really have no desire to hear the Truth
because the Truth would contradict the false beliefs by
which we live our life. Hence, those who are in self-love
tend to mock the literal stories of the Bible without affect-
ing its inner Truth.

The wall is "an hundred and forty-four cubits, the measure of a man, that is, of an angel" because all the Truths
and Goods of this city are derived from the Divine-Human
or Divine Form. When seen or perceived as a whole, Heav-
en appears holographically as a beautiful angel because
the form of an angel is in correspondence with the in-formation of Truth. The wall is made of jasper. Jasper is a
translucent gemstone that is able to let some light pass
through like the literal sense is able to convey the Spiritual
and Celestial senses.

The city or doctrine itself is made of pure spiritual gold
or Love unto pure spiritual glass which allows all Truth
from the Lord to flow in. The foundations of this doctrine
are adorned with precious stones because they are derived from the literal stories of the Word. The twelve
gates or introductory truths of this New Church consist of
the acknowledgment of the Lord as the Divine-Human,
the Truths of His Wisdom and the Goods of His Love. The
streets or ways by which the citizens of this city conduct

(walk) their lives are always in accordance with Love and Truth.

The Bible begins in the Garden of Eden or a state of Celestial innocent Love within the conceptual spaces of human consciousness. In this garden was the Tree of Life "And a river went out of Eden to water the garden; and from thence it was parted, and became into four heads." When man returns to Eden from his long spiritual journey, his heart becomes innocent again. However, this innocence does not spring from ignorance but from the wisdom of knowing that all the Good and Truth that is flowing into man's self by correspondence and influx originates in God:

> *And he showed me a pure river of water of life, bright as crystal, going forth from the throne of God and of the Lamb. In the midst of the street of it, and of the river, on this side and on that, was the tree of life, bearing twelve fruits, yielding its fruit every month; and the leaves of the tree were for the healing of the nations. And no accursed thing shall be there; and the throne of God and of the Lamb shall be in it, and His servants shall minister unto Him. And they shall see His face, and His name shall be in their foreheads. And there shall be no night there; and they have no need of a lamp and the light of the sun; for the Lord God giveth them light; and they shall reign for ages of ages.* Revelation 22: 1-5

The life of the Church is the result of its Truths and Heavenly doctrines. And this Truth originates from the Lord's throne or Heaven. The Lord's throne is Heaven and His footstool is the New Church. The Lord produces fruits or Goods within man when he intends and acts according to Truth. The leaves of the Tree of Life are the rational Truths that will enable those on Earth who are in evil and falsity to think rationally and to behave intelligently. These rational Truths will heal their minds and hearts. In the *New Jerusalem*, no one will be separated from the Lord because the Lord will reign in the conceptual spaces of the people's minds and hearts.

When humanity fell spiritually, it turned its back to God and began to live from self-love and self-intelligence. However, when the *New Jerusalem* will be established, human beings will turn around and see the face of God once again, "... and His name shall be in their foreheads." They will apprehend the qualities of His Love and Wisdom. In this New Church, faith will not be hypocritical. People will not be in the knowledge of God from self-pride or self-intelligence but from the real spiritual Light of His Word. And, in Heaven, the people will be conjoined with the Lord for eternity.

Chapter 10

NATURAL HEALING

If God is presently generating a New Heavenly Order within the conceptual spaces of our mind and a New Church in the physical spaces of our world through His universal attractor of Love, we should try to uncover how this restoration will unfold. On the natural level, we should expect that physical illnesses will be healed and most diseases will be eradicated. In society, injustice, violence and wars will subside and be gradually replaced by justice, usefulness, harmony and peace. On the mental level, false and irrational thoughts will be exchanged for rational and True ideas. And, on the spiritual level, evil lusts will be transformed into unselfish Love. This general healing will take place from humanity's understanding of the spiritual sense of the Word where the processes of reformation and regeneration are clearly explained.

We cannot understand the real causes of disease and the means of healing if we do not have a proper understanding of the real structure of the universe. We have seen that the whole universe, spiritual, mental and physical was generated from Divine Love. Divine Love consists of vortices arranged according to Divine Information or Truth. And this Truth is synonymous with the human form. But our biological body or physical organization is only displaying the effects of mental causes and spiritual purposes. Hence diseases are only effects or symptoms of our mental and spiritual discords.

Fig. 10.1. Rod of Asclepius and Caduceus of Hermes

If all things were derived from Divine Love, all things must be standing waves of energy. In the physical world, these objects are standing waves of physical energy and, in the conceptual realm, they are standing waves of emotional energy. We have seen how these standing waves consist of vortical spirals of involution and evolution on different scales. When the left and right-handed spirals of involution and evolution interfere constructively, they become harmonic conjugates and harmony, coherence, stability and health are established. Therefore, it is not a coincidence that the symbol of healing and medicine is the rod of Asclepius or the caduceus of Hermes (Fig. 10.1). In ancient myths, Asclepius was known as the god of healing and medicine while Hermes was the god of Wisdom. It is also evident that ancient civilizations possessed more real knowledge than we do now because these symbols are more than five thousand years old.

In order to understand what these symbols really mean, we must return to the Bible. In the Book of Numbers, there is a story that involves sin, disease and healing. While they are being led by Moses through the wilderness, the children of Israel become weary of their journey. They complain to Moses that they were happier in Egypt, where they could enjoy different varieties of food. They also begin to criticize God:

> And the people spake against God, and against Moses, Wherefore have ye brought us up out of Egypt to die in the wilderness? for there is no bread, neither is there any water; and our soul loatheth this light bread. And the Lord sent fiery serpents among the people, and they bit the people; and much people of Israel died. Therefore the people came to Moses, and said, We have sinned, for we have spoken against the Lord, and against thee; pray unto the Lord, that he take away the serpents from us. And Moses prayed for the people.

And the Lord said unto Moses, Make thee a fiery ser-
pent, and set it upon a pole: and it shall come to pass,
that every one that is bitten, when he looketh upon it,
shall live. And Moses made a serpent of brass, and put it
upon a pole, and it came to pass, that if a serpent had
bitten any man, when he beheld the serpent of brass,
he lived. Numbers 21: 5-9

Fig. 10.2. Moses Raising the Brass Serpent

When we sin, we lose God's Heavenly protection and
healing and the distorted fields of hell begin to manifest
in our life as physical disorder, accidents, and diseases.
Now, the interesting part of this story is how Moses heals
the people who are bitten by the poisonous serpents. The

symbol he manufactures is almost identical to the staff of Asclepius. The serpents in these ancient symbols are the spirals of involution and evolution of Love. It is also no co-incidence that they resemble the helices of DNA mole-cules that reside in the vortex centers or nuclei of our bio-logical cells. But these DNA molecules consist of atoms which are equally vortical (Fig. 10.3). Atoms must be vorti-cal because they consist of elementary particles (quarks) that are conjugates (quaternions). And these atoms of physical energy are in correspondence with vortical emo-tional energy in conceptual space.

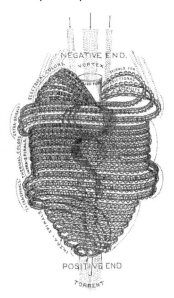

Fig. 10. 3. The Atom with its Spirals
and its Influx and Efflux Ethers (Babbitt)

PROPHECY

Almost 200 years before the helical structure of DNA was discovered, Swedenborg detected that the human will and understanding were organized vortically and these "vortex-like circlings" were the forms by which we could receive Life from God. Moreover, the quality of their organization determined the quality of a person's spiritual body and their spiritual destiny after death. Therefore, the vortices of our DNA are always in correspondence with the vortices of our will and mind. When we live in sin, our loves and beliefs become incoherent and they ultimately manifest as biological incoherence in our atoms and biological cells:

> *Every thing confirmed by the will and also by the understanding remains to eternity, because every one is his own love, and his love belongs to his will; also because every man is his own good or his own evil, for every thing that is called good, and likewise evil, belongs to the love. As man is his own love he is also a form of his love, and may be called the organ of his life's love. It has been said above, that the affections of the love and consequent thoughts of man are changes and variations of the state and form of the organic substances of his mind. What these changes and variations are and their nature shall now be explained. Some idea of them may be gathered from the heart and lungs, where there are alternate expansions and compressions or dilations and contractions, which in the heart are called systole and diastole and in the lungs respirations; these are a reciprocal distension and retraction or reciprocal*

stretching apart and closing together of their lobes. Such are the changes and variations of the state of the heart and lungs. There are like changes in the other viscera of the body, and changes more similar in their parts, by which the blood and the animal juice are received and carried onward.

Like things are to be found in the organic forms of the mind, which are the subjects of man's affections and thoughts, as has been shown above; with the difference that their expansions and compressions, or reciprocations, are relatively in such higher perfection as cannot be expressed in the words of natural language, but only in those of spiritual language, and these can be defined in no other way than that they are vortex-like circlings inward and outward, after the manner of perpetual and incurving spirals wonderfully bundled together into forms receptive of life.

The nature of these purely organic substances and forms in the evil and in the good shall now be stated. In the good these spiral forms are turned forward, but in the evil backward; and the spiral forms turning forward are turned towards the Lord and receive influx from Him, while those turning backward are turned towards hell and receive influx therefrom. It is to be known that so far as they are turned backward they are open behind and closed in front; and on the other hand, so far as they are turned forward they are opened in front and closed behind.

From all this it is evident what kind of a form or organ an evil man is, and what kind of a form or or-

gan a good man is, namely, that they are turned in contrary directions; and as the turning when once fixed cannot be reversed it is clear that such as man is when he dies such he remains to eternity. It is the love of man's will that makes the turning, that is, that converts and inverts, for, as has been said above, every man is his own love. It is from this that every man after death goes the way of his own love-he that is in a good love to heaven, and he that is in an evil love to hell, and he finds rest only in that society where his reigning love is; and what is wonderful, every one knows the way; it is like following a scent with the nose. (Swedenborg, Emanuel, *Divine Providence* (1764), #319, translated by John C. Ager, 1899)

Now, in order to discover how the children of Israel were healed by looking at the brass serpent, we must turn to the New Testament. We must also recall that Jesus (YHVH is salvation) came down to fulfill the Scriptures of the Old Testament. Therefore, this incident is a prophecy of what would occur after the Lord's crucifixion, glorification, resurrection and ascension. His body would become the body by which we would be able to heal:

And as Moses lifted up the serpent in the wilderness, even so must the Son of man be lifted up: That whosoever believeth in him should not perish, but have eternal life. John 3: 14-15

When God incarnated as the Messiah (Christ) on Earth, He glorified His human flesh and generated a Divine-Human body. This Divine-Human body is now able to heal any human who has faith in God. The serpent represents matter and sensuality. And raising the Son of Man means raising human flesh into the realm of spirit. The wings in the upper portion of the caduceus represent consciousness or spirit. When those people who were bitten by the poisonous serpents looked at the brass serpent, they were acknowledging God's power to heal through the body of of Jesus. We have ample evidence of this in the New Testament where Jesus is healing the sick. After they are healed, He always says: "Your faith has made you whole!" It is always our own faith in God's power that heals us.

Before we discover how faith in the Lord heals, we must first unravel how disease begins. Long before we are diagnosed with any serious illness and experience physical symptoms, we are emotionally unstable and experiencing negative thoughts. This is because physical illness is the result of mental and emotional discord. The natural realm only displays the effects of mental causes and spiritual purposes. And the state of our physical well-being is completely dependent upon the state of our consciousness. In figure 10.4, we can see that the human structure is essentially a vortex of emotional, mental and biological (vital) energy. We are continually receiving Love, Wisdom and Life from God. When we harmonically return or reciprocate this Love by loving intentions, wise thoughts and useful deeds in the world, the various energies within our whole being are able to properly circulate and keep us in a state of coherence, health and vitality.

However, when we live from self-love and self-intelligence, believe that existence is purely material, and
willfully refuse to reciprocate Love, we obstruct the flow
of coherent energy within our human organism. This is
how disease begins. Since our whole human organism
must be in correspondence with Heaven and our being is
a fractal chaotic system, physically, this connection occurs
at the plexi of our human organism.

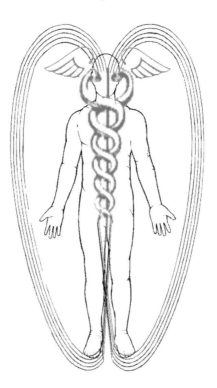

Fig.10.4. The Flow of Energy in the Human Organism

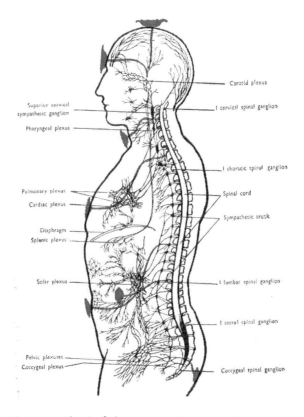

Fig. 10.5. Plexi of the Human Nervous System

For example, in figure 10.5 we can see the plexi of the nervous system. A plexus is where waves of energy interfere. When this interference is harmonic, energy is able to flow back into Heaven and the Love within our own being continues to grow. In Eastern traditions, these plexi are called *chakras*. There are essentially seven *chakras* by which energy from Heaven flows in and out of our human organism.

Now, many people speak about faith but very few understand what it means. In fact, many people continue to fulfill their selfish lusts, hate their neighbor and say that they believe in God. Some are also full of anxiety and fear and continue to pretend that they have faith. If we are in fear, we are not in faith:

> Angels have told me that the life of our dominant love never changes for anyone to all eternity because we are our love, so to change it in any spirit would be to take away and snuff out his or her life. They have also told me that this is because after death we can no longer be reformed by being taught the way we could in this world, since the outmost level, made up of natural insights and affections, is then dormant and cannot be opened because it is not spiritual. The deeper functions of our mind or spirit rest on this level the way a house rests on its foundation, which is why we do stay forever like the life of our love in the world. Angels are utterly amazed that people do not realize that our nature is determined by the nature of our dominant love and that many people actually believe they can be saved by instantaneous mercy, simply on the basis of their faith alone, regardless of the kind of life they have led, not realizing that divine mercy operates through means. The means involve being led by the Lord in the world as well as afterward in heaven, and the people who are led by mercy are the ones who do not live in evil. People do not

*even know that faith is an affection for what is true,
an affection that comes from a heavenly love that
comes from the Lord.*   (Swedenborg, Emanuel,
Heaven and Hell (1758), #480, translated by G. F.
Dole, 2000.)

If we live in fear and anxiety, it is because we do not really
believe that Heaven and God are real. We are in fact disconnected from Heaven and no longer receiving God's
loving protection and healing. To heal biologically, we
must in effect change what we love, what we believe and
how we live our life. When our faith is grounded in Love,
we are connected to the Lord's Divine-Human body and
able to receive His healing and protection. By looking at
the brass serpent, the children of Israel (Truth) perceived
how the Lord would heal the people by means of the Divine-Human body He would generate through His
incarnation as the Messiah (Christ) on earth.

In the beginning of this book, we unraveled how harmony is an infinite complexity that reconciles Order and
Chaos. This was in fact confirmed by Chaos theory and the
geometry of fractals. It turns out that even the beating of
our heart is the result of a harmony between Order and
Chaos. In order to understand how this harmony is produced, we must first understand the concept of a beat
frequency. When two waves of slightly different frequency interfere, they produce an interference pattern that
manifests as a beat or change in amplitude whose rate is
the difference between the two frequencies (Fig. 10.6). In
the case of the human heart, this interference is much
more complex and chaotic because our heart is an attrac-

tor or vortex where the waves of our own being interfere with the waves of the whole universe. We are even connected to Heaven and God through our heart and lungs. In fact, it is God who keeps our heart beating because He is the only source of Life in the universe.

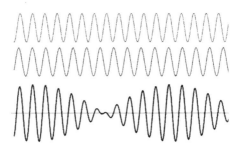

Fig. 10.6. Beat Frequency

It is also becoming increasingly evident that, like the human organism, harmony and peace in human society must be a delicate balance between Unity and Diversity, Freedom and Law, Order and Chaos. Political and social conflicts stem from humanity's lack of real Truth. As long as human beings believe that human life on earth is an end in itself, there will continue to be conflicts and wars. Physical gold may be valuable in the temporary realm of our short earthly existence but it is worthless in the eternal realm of our soul. What is the end of human physical life on Earth? It is physical death! Hence, physical gold will be useless to us when we die. The most valuable substance on Earth or natural gold must correspond to the most precious substance (energy) in Heaven, spiritual gold or Love. And, if we expect to enter the lavish, beautiful and pleasant estates of Heaven, instead of accumulating physical gold, we should be generating emotional gold or Love. We can carry this precious substance with us into the spiritual world because Love is spiritual and eternal.

The Earth was not designed by God to be a place where we fulfill our selfish desires and lusts; it was conceived to be an environment where we can exercise our freewill and rationality. And, by freely choosing to live a life of faith, love and usefulness, we would generate an eternal soul that has the capacity to subsist in the harmonic fields of Heaven. Human beings may have been granted spiritual Liberty by God. However, this Liberty is linked to a Responsibility. Order without Freedom is stagnation but Freedom without Responsibility is Chaos.

Over the ages, there has arisen an eternal conflict between those humans who endorse socialism and those who believe in individualism or capitalism. By itself, either one of these political systems will tend to degenerate into excess, the people will revolt and they will elect its opposite. This is what has already transpired throughout history in every nation. We must understand that this conflict is essentially a conflict between Chaos and Order, Freedom and Law. Spiritually, we have seen that Freedom and Law are always linked. In order to be *really* Free, we must obey the Laws of spiritual Life. And, when we transgress the Law, we automatically lose our Freedom and become entangled in the chaos of hell.

What is spiritually true must be equally true on our social level because humanity is linked by correspondence to
the spiritual world. In a healthy or harmonious society, every individual should be free to exercise his spiritual
liberty but equally responsible for the well-being of the
whole society. The civil Laws of such a society should reflect this Truth. And such a harmonious society can only
be realized if human beings are connected to the conceptual spaces of Heaven through rationality, faith,
usefulness and mutual Love.

Harmony is the essential definition of a chaotic fractal
because such a fractal is a whole consisting of parts that
are sufficiently free, unique and diverse to produce contrast while they are sufficiently similar to the whole to
produce order. The human body of organic cells is such a
fractal and so is Heaven which consists of angels and societies of angels all organized in the human form. When
human society on earth will be properly connected to
Heaven and God, it will also be transformed into such a
peaceful, beautiful and vibrant fractal. But this will require
a completely new vision of the universe, one that reconciles all human disciplines.

Chapter 11

MENTAL HEALING

In the last chapter, we concluded that physical and social healing have their source in mental and emotional
healing because the physical world of physical and biological energies is in correspondence with the conceptual
realm of our mental and emotional energy. And, in order
to generate a spiritual body that can reside in the conceptual and harmonic fields of Heaven, we must change our
mind and transform our will. In fact, we must generate a
New Mind and a New Will. This is what being "born again"
means. When the Lord descended as the Messiah on
Earth, most people did not understand what He really
meant by this saying because they interpreted what He
said literally. Even Nicodemus, one of the Pharisees, was
very puzzled:

Nicodemus saith unto him, How can a man be born when he is old? can he enter the second time into his mother's womb, and be born? Jesus answered, Verily, verily, I say unto thee, Except a man be born of water and of the Spirit, he cannot enter into the kingdom of God. That which is born of the flesh is flesh; and that which is born of the Spirit is spirit. Marvel not that I said unto thee, Ye must be born again. The wind bloweth where it listeth, and thou hearest the sound thereof, but canst not tell whence it cometh, and whither it goeth: so is every one that is born of the Spirit. John 3: 4-8

Like the wind is invisible, this birth cannot be seen because it is taking place within the conceptual spaces of our heart and mind. And, although this birth may be physically imperceptible, it is very real. In fact, we are generating a spiritual body that will consist of spiritual and mental energies that are eternal and will last forever. The conception and growth of this mental and spiritual body resembles the embryonic growth of a human organism. We know that a human being is conceived when a human female ovum is fertilized by a male sperm. In the same way, the love in our heart must be fertilized with Truth. Where can we find this Truth? When the Lord was physically on Earth, it proceeded directly from His mouth and the words He spoke. However, today we can continue to receive this Truth from the Word or Bible.

The love in our heart is the freewill that we have been granted by God from the beginning of time. Hence, in order to fertilize our heart with Truth, we must freely acknowledge and believe that God exists and that the Bible is His Truth. This is how our spiritual body is conceived. We should emphasize that it is conceived and not born yet. The fetus must develop and grow until it is ready to be born into the spiritual atmosphere. And we know that not all pregnancies are always successful. Some babies may also be stillborn. The parable of the sower in the New Testament describes the different ways humans receive Truth from the Lord. In order to successfully receive the Truth and use it to transform our mind, will and life, we must love it unconditionally.

When he was young, the enigmatic mystic, George I. Gurdjieff, noticed that human behavior was very strange. Human beings were rushing around driven by selfish desires like zombies. And the human mind seemed to have no integrity or real will. He desired to know the Truth about this human condition and no one could tell him what was the real purpose of human existence on Earth. He was then informed that there were some organizations or brotherhoods that had preserved the real Truth. His desire to find Truth was so intense that he immediately embarked with his friends on a perilous journey to find such a brotherhood. After overcoming many obstacles and enduring many struggles, he finally found what he was seeking. And, when he asked about this, he was told that human beings were behaving strangely and creating conflicts and wars because they were in a state of sleep or hypnosis. But how could they be physically awake, move physically, do all kinds of things and even drive automobiles if they were asleep? He was told that, while they were doing all this, they were not aware of themselves. In this state of hypnosis, their mind was fragmented or compartmentalized into many "I's" that did not know each other. When we are in the spiritual darkness of sleep, we do not feel the pangs and stings of conscience that result from experiencing the contradictions within our mind. Gurdjieff used the spiritual technique of *self-remembering* to begin to awaken.

We know that what Gurdjieff discovered is true because, in the Bible itself, we are told that God put Adam into a deep sleep. And, later, in the New Testament, we are urged to wake up from this spiritual sleep. This sleep is a kind of forgetfulness. Due to the fall of mankind, we have forgotten that we are connected to the spiritual world and God. To awaken from this spiritual sleep, we must become self-aware. Swedenborg communicated exactly the same thing when he said:

> *The state of a person when caught up in the pro-prium, that is, when he imagines that he lives from himself, is compared to a deep sleep. Indeed the ancients actually called it 'a deep sleep' while the Word speaks of people having 'the spirit of deep sleep poured out on them, and of their sleeping a perpetual sleep. The fact that man's proprium is in itself dead, that is, that nobody possesses any life from himself, has been demonstrated in the world of spirits so completely that evil spirits who love nothing except the proprium, and insist stubbornly that they*

do live from themselves, have been convinced by means of living experience, and have admitted that they do not live from themselves. With regard to the human proprium I have for several years now been given a unique opportunity to know about it - in particular that not a trace of my thinking began in myself. I have also been allowed to perceive clearly that every idea constituting my thought flowed in [from somewhere], and sometimes how it flowed in, and where from. Consequently anyone who imagines that he lives from himself is in error. And in believing that he does live from himself he takes to himself everything evil and false, which he would never do if what he believed and what is actually the case were in agreement. (Swedenborg, Emanuel, *Arcana Coelestia*, #150, translated by J. E. Elliott, 1983)

Happy is he that is awake, signifies the happy state of those who look to the Lord. This is evident from the signification of "happy," as being to be in a happy state; also from the signification of "being awake," as being to acquire for oneself spiritual life; and this is acquired by man's looking to the Lord, because the Lord is Life itself, and from Him alone is life eternal. When a man is in life from the Lord he is in wakefulness; but when he is in life from himself he is asleep; or what is the same, when a man is in spiritual life he is in wakefulness, but when he is in natural life separated from the spiritual he is asleep; and what a man then sees is like what he sees in a dream. To live this life is meant also by "sleeping and slumbering" in the Word (as in Matt. 13:25; 25:5, 6; Mark 4:26, 27;

13:36; Isa. 5:27; Jer. 51:39, 57; Ps. 13:4; 76:7; and else-where). *This makes clear what is signified by "being awake."* (Swedenborg, Emanuel, *Apocalypse Explained* (1759), #1006, translated by John White-head, 1911.)

To know that we are spiritually asleep is the beginning of our reformation. And whenever we act in the world, we should always remember that we are in connection with the spiritual world (Fig. 11.1). This means that all the selfish desires and false thoughts that are inflowing into us from hell are not our own. They emanate from the hereditary DNA of our human ancestors who fell into self-love and self-intelligence. We only make these falsehoods ours when we believe in them and we make these evil desires part of our own will when we put them into effect through evil actions in the world.

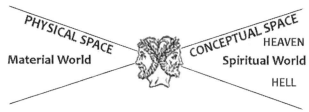

Fig. 11.1. Seeing in Physical Space
while Perceiving in Conceptual Space

It is also equally true that all the Wisdom and unselfish Love that inflows into us from Heaven is not ours. It is a free gift that belongs to the Lord alone. We have the right to use and share this Love and Truth but no right to possess it. We can reform our mind by understanding and be-lieving Truth and we can regenerate our will through lov-ing and useful works in the world. However, we should not attribute any Good and Truth to our self. Doing so would only inflate our ego with false-pride and arrogance and impede our spiritual transformation.

If human beings expect to enter a new era of healing, they must wake up to the spiritual realities of Heaven. This means that they must begin to erase all the false as-sumptions they have accumulated over the ages and be-gin to understand and believe Truth from the Word. The spiritual world may be invisible to our sight but it is per-ceivable with our mind and heart. Heaven consists of real emotional energies and conceptual forms and these ener-gies and forms are governed by scientific laws.

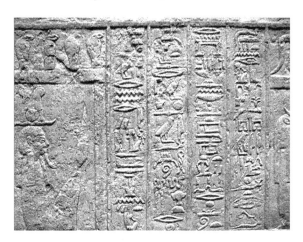

Fig. 11.2. Egyptian Graven Images
of what is in the Heavens

Fig. 11.3. Egyptian Pyramids and Sphinx

Before the ancient Egyptian civilization degraded into polytheism, idolatry and magic, it possessed the heavenly *science of correspondences*. We have direct evidence of this in archaeological artifacts and hieroglyphics (Fig. 11.2). The ancients knew that there was an eternal world that was in correspondence with the physical realm in which they existed. The pyramids point to a higher and eternal realm and the frail remains of the sphinx have withstood the ravages of time (Fig. 11.3).

It is also clearly evident by their statues and pic-tographs that the ancient Egyptians originally understood what *raising the serpent* meant, although this knowledge became corrupted when they started to worship idols (Fig. 11.4). The serpent represents coiled energy in the base of the human spine. In the unregenerate, this energy is sensual. It is a desire for what is material and a sexual desire to procreate. However, when this energy is spiritualized, it uncoils, organizes harmonically, ascends and transforms into higher mental and spiritual energy. The sexual desire to procreate is then transformed into the urge to regenerate or to realize Truth and Good.

Fig. 11.4. Egyptian Statue of Khonsu

It is known, that in Egypt there were hieroglyphics, and that they were inscribed on the columns and walls of the temples and other buildings; and that no one at this day is able to determine their signification. Those hieroglyphics were no other than the correspondences of natural and spiritual things, to which science the Egyptians more than any people in Asia applied themselves, and according to which the oldest peoples of Greece formed their fables; for this, and this only, was the most ancient style of composition; to which I will add this new information, that all things seen by spirits and angels in the spiritual world are solely correspondences; and the whole Sacred Scripture is on this account written by correspondences, that by it, because it is such, it might be the means of conjunction between the men of the church and the angels of heaven. But as the Egyptians, and with them the people of the kingdoms of Asia, began to convert these correspondences into idolatries, to which the sons of Israel were prone, these latter were forbidden to make any use of them. This is evident from the first commandment of the Decalogue, which says:-

Thou shalt not make unto thee any graven image, nor any likeness of what is in the heavens above, or that is in the earth beneath, or that is in the waters under the earth. Thou shalt not bow down thyself to them, nor serve them, for I Jehovah am thy God (Deut. v. 8, 9).

Besides many passages elsewhere. From that time, the science of correspondences became obliterated, and successively to such an extent, that at this day it is scarcely known that it ever existed, and that it is anything. (Swedenborg, Emanuel, *The White Horse (1758)*, translated by John Whitehead, 1892)

The *Egyptian Book of the Dead* is literally called "The Book of Emerging forth into the Light." The ancient Egyptians believed that a human being's soul continued to exist after death. This soul was first taken into the Light of God (Osiris). After this initial encounter, it had to undergo a spiritual judgment in which the soul's heart was weighed on a scale against the feather of Maat (Truth). If the scales were in balance, it meant that the human being in question had lived a life in accordance with conscience and reason and the soul would be able to continue its long journey to the "Field of Reeds." Such a soul would then enter into these spiritual and eternal paradisaical fields through well-guarded gates. However, if a soul's heart were heavy with evil, it would cause the scales of Justice to tip and indicate that such a person had lived an evil life motivated by selfishness. Such a soul, by the heaviness of its sins, would then automatically fall into an abyss of spiritual darkness.

Now, the reason we are interested in Egyptian life after death is to show that the descriptions of the afterlife of all true religions are essentially identical. The existence of life after death is equally well-documented by many individuals who have undergone near-death experiences. Swedenborg was able to witness this transition of human beings after death. And he equally confirmed that there are gates that open into both Heaven and hell. More importantly, he detected that a human soul was only attracted and could only perceive the gates that were in exact correspondence with its state of being. Those who were in Truth and Love were attracted by the gates of Heaven while those who were in falsehood and evil were overwhelmed and repulsed by Heavenly Light and attracted by the obscure environments of hell.

In order to understand and believe the Word of God or Bible, it is necessary to believe in life after death. Otherwise, the symbolic meaning of the Bible is useless and the parables and teachings of Jesus are meaningless. The Kingdom of Heaven is within us because it subsists in the conceptual spaces of our mind. Our mind is rational because it evolved in correspondence with the rational proportions of Heaven. It is by means of this mind that we are eventually able to enter the harmonic fields of Heaven. And it is by our understanding of the Word of God that we are affiliated with angels and conjoined with Heaven and the Lord:

> It has been made plain to me by much experience that the spiritual angels are in the spiritual sense of the Word, and the celestial angels in its celestial sense. While reading the Word in its sense of the letter it has been given me to perceive that communication was effected with the heavens, now with this society of them, now with that, and that what I understood according to the natural sense, the spiritual angels understood according to the spiritual sense, and the celestial angels according to the celestial sense, and this in an instant. As I have perceived this communication many thousands of times, there remains with me no doubt about it. (Swedenborg, Emanuel, Doctrine of Sacred Scripture (1763), #64, translated by John F. Potts, 1904)

.... the Word has been given by the Lord to man and also to the angels in order that by it they may be with Him; for the Word is the medium that unites earth with heaven, and through heaven with the Lord. Its literal sense is that which unites man with the first heaven; and as within the literal there is an internal sense which treats of the Lord's kingdom, and within this a supreme sense which treats of the Lord; and as these senses are in order one within another, it is evident what is the nature of the union with the Lord that is effected by means of the Word. (Swedenborg, Emanuel, *Arcana Coelestia* (1756), #3476, translated By john Potts, 1965)

The Word is not understood, except by those who are enlightened. The human rational faculty cannot comprehend Divine, nor even spiritual things, unless it be enlightened by the Lord. Thus they only who are enlightened comprehend the Word. The Lord enables those who are enlightened to understand truths, and to discern those things which appear to contradict each other. The Word in its literal sense appears inconsistent, and in some places seems to contradict itself. And therefore by those who are not enlightened, it may be so explained and applied, as to confirm any opinion or heresy, and to defend any worldly and corporeal love.

They are enlightened from the Word, who read it from the love of truth and good, but not they who read it from the love of fame, of gain, or of honor, thus from the love of self. They are enlightened who are in the good of life, and thereby in the affection of truth. They are enlightened whose internal is open, thus who as to their internal man are capable of elevation into the light of heaven. Enlightenment is an actual opening of the interiors of the mind, and also an elevation into the light of heaven. There is an influx of holiness from the internal, that is, from the Lord through the internal, with those who regard the Word as holy, though they themselves are ignorant of it.

They are enlightened, and see truths in the Word, who are led by the Lord, but not they who are led by themselves. They are led by the Lord, who love truth because it is truth, who also are they that love to live according to Divine truths. The Word is vivified with man according to the life of his love and faith. The things derived from one's own intelligence have no life in themselves, because from man's proprium there is nothing good. They cannot be enlightened who have much confirmed themselves in false doctrine. (Swedenborg, Emanuel, *The White Horse* (1758), #7, translated by John Whitehead, 1892)

The rational level is the lowest level of the human spiritual mind. And when we confine our understanding to natural matter, space and time, our mind is shut to the spiritual realities of Heaven. This is what happened after man's spiritual downfall. Man fell into self-love and self-intelligence and started to believe that reality is material. As a result, he lost touch with the spiritual realities of Heaven. It is also rather astounding that today's scientists, as rational and intelligent as they are, have absolutely no contact with the realities of the conceptual spaces of their mind. Many of today's scientists are atheists, believe only in nature and assume that intelligence is the sole result of quantum gravity. And, although they continue to develop theories of matter that involve many dimensions and countless virtual particles, they categorically refuse to even suspect that these dimensions may be states of conceptual mind and spirit. According to physicists, the fundamental units of matter or *quarks* come in different *flavors* such as *up, down, strange, charm, top* and *bottom*. Is strangeness or charm a physical quality? Quarks have these conjugate qualities because the physical world is being generated from the conceptual world. And we have seen that quaternions, octonions, sedenions and hypernumbers have no physical units; they have no mass, no charge and no time because they describe the harmonic relationships that exist within the conceptual spaces of Love and Wisdom. When he was conscious in the spiritual realm, Swedenborg was also astonished by the number of people who believe that nature created the universe out of nothing:

> At one point I was struck with amazement at the vast number of people who attribute creation - everything under the sun and everything beyond it as well - to nature. No matter what they see, they say with heartfelt conviction, "Surely this is nature's doing."

I have asked them why they say nature is responsible for everything, and why not God, especially since they repeatedly use the common expression, "God created nature," and therefore could as easily say that God, rather than nature, is responsible for what they see. Beneath their breath, in an almost inaudible voice, they reply, "What God is there except nature?"

Their conviction that the universe was created by nature - an insanity that seems like wisdom to them - makes them all feel so glorious that they look down on all who acknowledge that the universe was created by God. They picture these faithful people as ants that crawl on the ground and tread a well-worn path. Some they picture as butterflies that flit around in the air. "Dreams" - that is what they call the dogmas of the faithful, who see what they themselves do not see. "Who has seen God?" they say; "Who has not seen nature?"

While I stood amazed at the vast number of such people, an angel appeared at my side and said, "What are you thinking about?"

I replied, "I'm thinking about the vast number of people who believe that nature exists from itself - that nature itself created the universe."

"All hell is made up of such people," the angel told me. "There they are called satans and devils. The satans are those who have come to deny the existence of God because they have convinced themselves to believe in nature. The devils are those whose ac-

*knowledgment of God has been driven from their
hearts because they have spent their lives commit-
ting crimes. "* (Swedenborg, Emanuel, *True Christian
Religion*, #35, translated by J. Rose, 2010)

When we only believe our natural senses and ascribe
all beauty, structure and order to nature, our mind may be
rational but we are in spiritual darkness. As a result, we
also assume the universe has no meaning or purpose. A
purely material universe cannot have any meaning because meaning originates in the realm of ideas. Chaos, by
itself, would be a void of darkness but Chaos is given
meaning by the Word of God, Divine Order or Truth. We
have seen that Divine Love is an infinitely complex harmony between Chaos and Order, Freedom and Law. "In the
beginning was the Word (Divine Order) and the Word was
with God (Divine Love) and the Word was God." Order or
meaning is embedded within the fractal generator and attractor of Divine Love and, as this fractal attractor generates the universe, its Order gives meaning and structure
to every being in creation:

*For God to love or desire a world was to give that
world substance, or being; for God to think that
world which He desired was to give it form. The
Word is the spoken thought. The beginning of the
world was the spoken thought of God. This is the
"Let there be light! " at which a visible and beautiful
world springs into being out of chaos and darkness.
While things are in darkness, it is as if they were not.
It is as the light appears that they take shape, and*

have a definite, cognizable existence. The mass of clay before the artist is as chaos; the idea broods over it, and breathes itself into it, like the Spirit of the Creator over the face of the deep. The Word, the forming idea, goes from the artist into the clay, moulding that into form which had no form, and making each part to be a related part, or part of a whole; thus distinguished from, at the same time that it is united to, other parts. In this way a new thing is created which, without this living Word, had never been; and so the statue stands forth complete — a form of beauty, of harmony, of "parts" and "relations" — things purely ideal; and so expressing the mind and the dream of the artist. So did the creative Word of God give to each thing in nature its distinctive being.

"Without Him was not anything made that was made." It is the Divine Wisdom going forth from the Divine Love that put form, and thus a meaning into nature, and made it in any sense a book. It is not uncommon for scientists to speak of the "meaning" of nature. But surely there can be no meaning in nature but that which was put there. Nature, as unintelligent force, could not have blindly shaped itself to have a "meaning," and then the meaning have come in, or rather come out, as an after-thought or accident. But meaning is a thing of mind, and a "meaning in nature " is nothing else than "mind in nature," i. e. the Word as Creator. For a book is only what has words, and nature is a book only as it contains the Words, the expressed ideas, of its Maker. To the eye *of the brute, a book is not a book of words; it is a lump of matter. So to the naturalist, who sees in nature no wisdom or intelligence written in words — to such a mind nature is no book; it is sheer bulk. To him, nature is as yet truly without form, and void : it has not yet been touched by the creative Word.* (Sewall, Frank, *The New Metaphysics*, James Speirs, London, 1888.)

Therefore, in order to discover the meaning and purpose of nature, we must understand the Word of God. As we read and attempt to understand the Bible's *Spiritual* and *Celestial* senses, our mind is being restructured, restored and healed by the Lord's Wisdom. However, it is only by living a life in accordance with this Wisdom that we can continue to heal our mind. Our understanding and beliefs are derived from our will. And our will is who we really are because we become who we are by what we freely intend and do in the world. We can use our rational mind to understand Truth but we can equally misuse and abuse it to rationalize our selfish and cruel intentions and actions. This is the choice that we compelled to make every day that we live on Earth. The material level of the Earth is the only place where we are able to freely choose what we love and believe. And, after we die physically, we will be attracted by the spiritual environments that correspond exactly to our loves and beliefs.

When we read and understand the Word, the angels of Heaven are able to communicate with us in the conceptual spaces of our mind. In order to understand how this is accomplished, we must understand what real thoughts or ideas represent. If the conceptual realm is real, ideas must be real forms of energy in our mind. When we hear a spoken word, this word enters our ears as sound waves of energy. These waves are then decoded as a mental image in our mind by correspondence. Now, in the case of natural objects such as the word "elephant" for example, the mental image is very straightforward. We perceive the form of an *ideal* elephant in our mind. However, with abstract concepts such as "justice," we may perceive a whole series of conceptual images in our mind.

In the world, people with different native languages may not be able to communicate. However, since the structure of the human mind is universally similar, in the spiritual world, all beings are able to communicate through conceptual ideas and their representatives. The angels are continually projecting True ideas into our mind. And these ideas are automatically converted into our own native language by correspondence. This is how angels speak to us. in the conceptual world, all beings are able to communicate by representatives or the universal language of correspondences:

> *Furthermore spirits and angels communicate everything to others by means of representatives. By means of wonderful variations of light and shade they bring their own thoughts in a vivid way before the internal sight and at the same time before the external sight of the one with whom they are communicating, and subtly introduce those thoughts by effecting appropriate changes in his affectional state. The representations manifested in their communica-*

tions with others are not like those described already, but they are produced without delay and in an instant, together with the ideas conveyed in their communications. It is like a lengthy description of something, accompanied at the same time by the presentation before the eyes of a visual image of that thing. For amazing as it is, by means of varying kinds of images that are quite beyond man's comprehension any spiritual reality at all can be set forth in representative form in which inwardly there are things that go with the perception of truth, and still more inwardly those that go with the perception of good.

Such things also exist within man - for man is a spirit clothed with the body - as becomes clear from the fact that when anything spoken that is perceived by the ear rises up towards the more interior parts, it passes into mental images not unlike those of visual objects, and from these into conceptual ideas, and in this way one comes to perceive the sense of the words. Anyone who reflects on these matters properly may recognize from them that within him there is his spirit, which is his internal man, and also that he has this kind of ability to communicate following his separation from the body, for the same ability exists with him though this is not evident to him in his lifetime because of the obscurity, indeed the thick darkness brought about by earthly, physical, and worldly things. (Swedenborg, Emanuel, *Arcana Coelestia*, #3342, translated by J. E. Elliott, 1983)

It is by this same process that we access the realities of Heaven when we read and understand the Word. In the beginning, the spiritual level of our mind may be completely closed and we may only understand the word literally. However, as we progressively learn the spiritual correspondence of each word, our spiritual mind will start to open up and we will understand the real meaning of the Bible. We will then realize that the whole natural world is a book that is filled with meaning. Precious stones in the world are representative of these literal Bible stories that allow the Light of Divine Truth to pass into our mind. The trees, plants and beautiful flowers that uplift our spirit in the world are the knowledges of Truth that reside in our memory. The charming birds that adorn the spaces of our physical atmosphere correspond to the pleasant thoughts that fly in the conceptual spaces of our mind. Finally, the gentle deer, sheep, goats and cattle that feed on the green pastures of the land are the innocent affections or emotional energies that constitute Heaven.

We obtain the natural knowledge of the physical world through natural science. But we receive the spiritual knowledge of conceptual and spiritual realities from Divine Revelation. The City of God or New Jerusalem descends from Heaven and into our mind through Divine Revelation:

> *The purpose of revelation is the salvation of the world, with all that this implies. It is, therefore, a new genesis, or a creating of a new world out of a moral chaos. It is redemption, and to this end, the Word made flesh, suffering, triumphing and ascending in*

glory. It is the coming of the Lord to judgment. It is the City of God. It is the permanent presence and indwelling of God with men. In a word, the Creator of the world is its Saviour! and becomes so by revelation. The Father of man REVEALS Himself to His child. God as unknown and inconceivable is not the heavenly Father. No rational conception of God can admit that He created intelligent souls only for ever to evade their knowledge, to hide Himself from their recognition and their love. The father reveals himself to his child. God the Father of all reveals Himself to His immortal creatures in His Word, which is His Wisdom. By means of His Word made flesh He, as the Divine Truth, clothes Himself with human nature, and Himself comes down to the low estate of us men, to redeem and save us. The Father of men, in His revealings of Himself to man, is Life, the life of the Father's love, and that life is thus become the "Light of men." The Creator of the world thus becomes its Preserver, its Saviour. The salvation He procures by means of His Word is the restoration of human souls to the laws of His own Divine Order — the laws of a blessed, an eternal, heavenly life.

This is the full, round plan of God's Providence as the end of creation. To create a world is not enough to answer the ends of an infinite love, if creation is not followed by salvation. The end of the creation of the world is that a heaven of angels, who have first been men on earth, may enjoy to eternity the gifts of the heavenly Father's love, and reciprocate this love in love and service to one another. This end or pur-

pose would have been realized in the first creation, the first genesis, had not mankind, by the abuse of free will and rationality, become the father of evil, and thence of the disease and disorder, the misery and strife that come from breaking the laws of a perfect Creator. To restore human life to order, to make it possible for man freely to return to the life of heaven and to become that immortal angel of light, and beauty, and power that God first designed him — for this Redemption was necessary, and for this the Lord became man. The Divine becomes now the Sender and the Sent. The Love is what sends; the Truth, or Word, is what is sent. ("That the world may know that Thou hast sent me, and hast loved them" St. John xvii. 23) The Divine becomes now the Father and the Son. The Father is the Love that sends; the Son is the Truth, the Word, that is sent. Truth is the messenger of the gospel, but its message is Love. The Truth, the Word, of God is made flesh, and we behold His glory, the glory of the only begotten of the Father, the glory of the Divine Wisdom begotten of the Divine Love — full of grace and truth. (Sewall, Frank, *The New Metaphysics*, James Speirs, London, 1888.)

God proved that His love for the whole human race is infinite and unconditional by coming down in the flesh, restoring spiritual equilibrium and paving a spiritual way for us to return into Heaven. By understanding the inmost or *Celestial* sense of the Word, we discover how much God loves and cares for us. On the Celestial level, the whole

Bible concerns the Lord because the Lord IS the Word or Divine Truth. In the New Testament, this is obvious but, in the Old Testament, this may not be immediately apparent. However, when we delve into the deeper meaning, we begin to see the Light.

Since the Old Testament was written before the Gospels, in the Celestial sense, the stories of the Old Testament mostly embed prophecies and information regarding the Lord's coming into the world as the Messiah (Christ). This is in fact why Jesus said that He came to fulfill the Scriptures. For example, the call of Abram is an account of the Lord's childhood. All the details in these stories are exact correspondences of what would be taking place within the Lord's mind and heart in His infancy. And, although the story of Isaac's sacrifice, on the literal level, seems rather obscure, on the Celestial level, it becomes meaningful and prophetic. Isaac was the son of Abraham and Jesus was the Son (Divine Truth) of God (Divine Love). Like Isaac carried the wood by which he was to be sacrificed as a burnt-offering, Jesus carried His wooden cross by which He was crucified.

The story of Joseph is also a perfect example of this Celestial correspondence. Joseph was a shepherd and Jesus was the Good Shepherd. Joseph was betrayed by his brother Judah for twenty pieces of silver and the Lord was betrayed by His disciple Judas for thirty pieces of silver. Joseph was stripped of his coat of many colors when he was sold into slavery and the Lord was stripped of his garment when he was crucified. Joseph was imprisoned with two criminals, one of whom was saved and the Lord was crucified with two criminals, one of whom He saved. Joseph stored grain to feed the people in Egypt and the Lord fed the multitude. Joseph was reunited with his brothers and father in Egypt and the Lord was reunited with His disciples and Father (Divine Love) after His resurrection.

Fig. 11. 5. Elijah Ascending into Heaven
in a Chariot of Fire

Another prophecy of God descending as the Messiah on Earth is embedded in the story of Elijah and Elisha. When the prophet Elijah is in the process of departing this world, his disciple Elisha perceives this in an amazing spiritual vision where Elijah is taken up to Heaven in a chariot of fire (Fig. 11.5):

> And it came to pass, as they still went on, and talked, that, behold, there appeared a chariot of fire, and horses of fire, which parted them both asunder; and Elijah went up by a whirlwind into heaven. And Elisha saw it, and he cried, My father, my father, the chariots of Israel and the horsemen thereof! And he saw him no more: and he took hold of his own clothes, and rent them in two pieces. He took up also the mantle of Elijah that fell from him, and went back, and stood by the bank of the Jordan. And he took the mantle of Elijah that fell from him, and smote the waters, and said, Where is Jehovah, the God of Elijah? and when he also had smitten the waters, they were divided hither and thither; and Elisha went over. And when the sons of the prophets that were at Jericho over against him saw him, they said, The spirit of Elijah doth rest on Elisha. And they came to meet him, and bowed themselves to the ground before him. 2 Kings 2:11-15

Fire corresponds to Love, horses to understanding and a chariot to doctrines of Truth. Thus, we discover that Elijah, due to his love and understanding of Truth is directly lifted up into Heaven by a whirlwind or vortex of Divine Love. Although this is very revealing, it is not the most amazing part of this vision! The interesting part is hidden in the names of these two prophets. In Hebrew, Elijah or ELIYAHU means "My God is YAHU or YHVH" and Elisha, as in YEHOSHUA or Jesus, means "My God is Salvation." And if persons in the Bible represent elements of human and Divine Character, we can see how this story is another prophecy of God descending as the Messiah on Earth to save and heal His people. Like God [Father] descended as the Word [the Son] in the world, Elijah's mantle [Divine Truth] fell from Heaven into the world. Elisha tore the garments which he wore and put on Elijah's mantle [Divine Truth] like Jesus redeemed and glorified the corrupted humanity which He embodied through His human temptations. And, in fact, like Jesus, the prophet Elisha went on to heal many people.

Today, the Lord is once again revealing Himself by means of His Word. Through *Spiritual* and *Celestial* correspondences, we are seeing His power and glory:

> *The New Jerusalem, descending from God out of heaven; what is this but another and a final beginning, in which the Word is again the Creator of a new heaven and a new earth? Is it not the beginning of a new world, a new age, now that the old is passing away — a new world, morally, spiritually, intellectually? Is not the Word, the formative wisdom and reason of God, making over the mental world to-day in a new revelation of itself to man? And is not this new revelation such that when received it must abide; that " its sun shall never go down; " that its dominion must be an everlasting dominion, and its kingdom that which shall not pass away? Is it not, therefore, the permanent dwelling of God with man? has not the Word at length become actually and finally the*

presence of God upon the earth? (Sewall, Frank, *The New Metaphysics*, James Speirs, London, 1888.)

Chapter 12

SPIRITUAL HEALING

The New Jerusalem is harmonically proportioned according to the Golden ratio of Truth and it is made of gold. But this gold is not natural; it is spiritual. Spiritual gold is Love. And Love is a real emotional energy that is organized according to Truth. In the future, human beings on Earth will require a new will. Therefore, once we have repented and reformed our mind, we must regenerate our will. This process is much more difficult and extensive because our will is who we really are. We obtain our sense of self from our free loves and beliefs. To change our will is to be literally transformed. And we must undergo this process gradually in collaboration with God because it is God within us who is doing the spiritual healing.

When human beings will begin to understand the real purpose of their existence on Earth, they will recognize that healing in the world can only be the result of mental and spiritual healing. When we no longer cherish natural gold and self-glory and, instead, value the Love of our heart and the Truth of our mind, we are seeing the *New Jerusalem* descend on Earth. Spiritual healing is the education of our will because only what we love from the freedom of our will is who and what we are. It was only Swedenborg who recognized the importance and significance of the human will:

1. Love or the will is man's very life.

2. Love or the will strives unceasingly towards the human form and all things of that form.

3. Love or the will is unable to effect anything by its human form without a marriage with wisdom or the understanding.

4. Love or the will prepares a house or bridal chamber for its future wife, which is wisdom or the understanding.

5. Love or the will also prepares all things in its human form, that it may act conjointly with wisdom or the understanding.

6. After the nuptials, the first conjunction is through affection for knowing, from which springs affection for truth.

7. The second conjunction is through affection for understanding, from which springs perception of truth.

8. The third conjunction is through affection for seeing truth, from which springs thought.

9. Through these three conjunctions love or the will is in its sensitive life and in its active life.

10. Love or the will introduces wisdom or the understanding into all things of its house.

11. Love or the will does nothing except in conjunction with wisdom or the understanding.

12. Love or the will conjoins itself to wisdom or the understanding, and causes wisdom or the understanding to be reciprocally conjoined to it.

13. Wisdom or the understanding, from the potency given to it by love or the will, can be elevated, and can receive such things as are of light out of heaven, and perceive them.

14. Love or the will can in like manner be elevated and can perceive such things as are of heat out of heaven, provided it loves its consort in that degree.

15. Otherwise love or the will draws down wisdom or the understanding from its elevation, that it may act as one with itself.

16. Love or the will is purified by wisdom in the understanding, if they are elevated together.

17. Love or the will is defiled in the understanding and by it, if they are not elevated together.

18. Love, when purified by wisdom in the understanding, becomes spiritual and celestial.

19. *Love, when defiled in the understanding and by it, becomes natural and sensual.*

20. *The capacity to understand called rationality, and the capacity to act called freedom, still remain.*

21. *Spiritual and celestial love is love towards the neighbor and love to the Lord; and natural and sensual love is love of the world and love of self.*

22. *It is the same with charity and faith and their conjunction as with the will and understanding and their conjunction.* (Swedenborg, Emanuel, *Divine Love and Wisdom* (1763), #398, translated by John C. Ager, 1890)

Our mind is reformed through repentance but our will is re-generated through spiritual temptation. Now, we know fully well that the world in which we exist physically is a harsh, hazardous and uncertain environment. And we may experience many difficulties in the world that test the strength, integrity and resilience of our character. But this is not necessarily spiritual temptation. We may even live a moral life and not be conjoined with Heaven. If our life is still rooted in self-love and love of the world, it is completely natural and there is no conflict within us. However, when our mind is reformed and we acknowledge and believe Truth, a conflict arises within our being between what we now believe to be True and our natural desires. Spiritual temptation is a conflict or battle between what is spiritual and natural within us.

There is no story that illustrates the difficulty of changing our will as well as the story of Peter, Jesus' disciple, in the New Testament. Peter represents the rock of Truth or faith on which the Lord was to build His Church. But faith without Love is useless and insubstantial like the hypocritical faith that is practiced today. When we acknowledge and believe Truth from the Word, this Truth is still only in our mind or intellect; it is not yet in our heart or will. Hence, instead of finding fault with our self, we tend to project these faults onto others:

> It is a remarkable fact that it is easy for any one to rebuke another who is intending evil, and say to him, "Do not do this, because it is a sin," and yet it is difficult for him to say the same to himself. For in the latter case it is a matter of will, but in the former a matter of thought, easily communicated because very superficial. (Swedenborg, Emanuel, True Christian Religion (1770), #535, translated by W. C. Dick, 1950)

Hence, when Truth only resides in our mind, we may start to erroneously believe that we are morally superior. We may think that we are a very righteous person and begin to see the speck in other people's eye while we have a beam in our own eye. This was the case with the Pharisees whom Jesus rebuked. Since He was omniscient, Jesus could clearly see the state of every person's soul, and not just how they appeared to the world. We may fool the whole world but we can never deceive God. Jesus also knew the state of being of every one of His disciples because they were specifically chosen to represent the twelve qualities of human nature. During the Last Supper, Jesus tells His disciples that they will all betray Him. However, Peter answers that he would rather die than betray Him:

> *Peter answered and said unto him, Though all men shall be offended because of thee, yet will I never be offended. Jesus said unto him, Verily I say unto thee, That this night, before the cock crow, thou shalt deny me thrice. Peter said unto him, Though I should die with thee, yet will I not deny thee. Likewise also said all the disciples.* Matthew 26: 33-35

Of course, later in the narrative, we discover that the Lord's prophecy regarding Peter is completely fulfilled and he denies knowing Him on three occasions (or completely). Like most of us, Peter did not really know the true state of his soul. We are not what we say or believe ourselves to be; we are what we freely love, intend and do. Our will is who really are. Hence, we may acknowledge and believe Truth and still be unable to enter the harmonic fields of Heaven. In order to enter Heaven, we require a will that has been harmonized with Truth. And the process of transforming our will is lengthy, stressful and arduous.

Spiritual temptation must be undergone gradually and over a long period of time because human beings are not robots. They must change their will freely and progressively. If we were to transform our will instantly, we would lose our sense of self or who we freely are. But when we do this step by step, we are able to continue to function in the world without drastic transformation. It is only after many years or even decades of resisting temptation that we will notice that we have actually become a new person.

Now, what happened after the cock crowed the third time? It is important to recall the whole story because it illustrates exactly the nature of spiritual temptation:

> Now Peter sat without in the palace: and a damsel came unto him, saying, Thou also wast with Jesus of Galilee. But he denied before them all, saying, I know not what thou sayest. And when he was gone out into the porch, another maid saw him, and said unto them that were there, This fellow was also with Jesus of Nazareth. And again he denied with an oath, I do not know the man. And after a while came unto him they that stood by, and said to Peter, Surely thou also art one of them; for thy speech bewrayeth thee. Then began he to curse and to swear, saying, I know not the man. And immediately the cock crew. And Peter remembered the word of Jesus, which said unto him, Before the cock crow, thou shalt deny me thrice. And he went out, and wept bitterly. Matthew 26: 69-75

It is only through spiritual temptation that we are able to see who we really are. And when we perceive who we are in reality, we are shocked and grieved. This is not who we thought we were. We can only enter the Kingdom of God if we are able to do God's will. And God's will is unselfish Love. In order to follow the Lord and enter His

Kingdom we require the lamp of Faith; but a lamp without oil is useless. Love without Faith is not True Love, and Faith without Love is not Real Faith. The form of Love is Faith and the substance of Faith is Love:

"They that were foolish took their lamps, but took no oil with them." Oil, which is warm and smooth, represents the love-principle. In the lamp, the light is from the oil, not from the lamp, itself. The lamp is only the means of using the oil, to make light. So the lamp represents the doctrine, the knowledge, which, if filled with the warm oil of love, is a means of enlightenment and of intelligence. We see the character of oil, in its frequent use in the temple-service, in Israel.

But an empty lamp represents empty doctrine, doctrine held intellectually, only, and not filled with the love of good and truth; and hence, not carried out in the practical life. The oil of love feeds the light of spiritual intelligence, but the knowledge which is empty of love cannot maintain genuine intelligence.

The wise are those who receive the truth into their will as well as into their understanding; they take oil to keep their lamps supplied: their love of good and truth maintains their spiritual intelligence. The wise have both religious knowledge and religious life; they know the doctrine, and they keep the commandments; they have a pure heart, an enlightened understanding, and a holy life. The foolish have knowledge, but they do not shun evils, as sins.

(Mitchell, Edward Craig, *Parables of the New Testament Explained*, 1887)

Scientifically, we can only exist in a certain atmosphere if we possess the requisite substance and form to exist in such an atmosphere. For example, the only reason we are able to exist on planet Earth is because our physical body evolved in correspondence with its atmosphere. We need to breathe oxygen from the air and drink water to survive. If we could travel to Mars for instance, we would not be able to exist there. When astronauts went to the Moon, they needed to wear a heavy suit that isolated them from its harsh environment. Their existence on the Moon was not natural; it was artificial and temporary. Our form is also in correspondence with our function in the environment in which we live. For example, fish have evolved fins to swim in the oceans and birds have developed wings to fly in the air. Human beings have evolved feet to walk on the earth and hands to do useful tasks but they have equally evolved a mind to understand Truth and a will to freely intend what is Good. This is because they are generating an emotional, mental and vital body that will be able to subsist in the harmonic spiritual atmospheres of Heaven. Heaven is a real place (state) made of real substance (Love), organized in a real form (Truth). It is populated by real societies of real beings. And these beings or angels have real bodies.

There is really nothing abstract about spirituality. The laws of the spiritual world are just as scientific as those of the physical world. When our spiritual body disengages from the material level, it will simply seek and find a spiritual environment that matches it as closely as possible. This is because we can only be comfortable in an environment that matches our dominant love. And, if we desire to be in Heaven, we need to develop a loving will through spiritual temptation:

> *A great deal of my experience has testified to the fact that we are our love or intention after death. All heaven is differentiated into communities on the basis of differences in the quality of love, and every spirit who is raised up into heaven and becomes an angel is taken to the community where her or his love is. When we arrive there we feel as though we are in our own element, at home, back to our birthplace, so to speak. Angels sense this and associate there with kindred spirits. When they leave and go somewhere else, they feel a constant pull, a longing to go back to their kindred and therefore to their dominant love. This is how people gather together in heaven. The same applies in hell. There too, people associate according to loves that oppose heavenly ones.*
>
> *We may also gather that we are our love after death from the fact that anything that does not agree with our dominant love is then removed and apparently taken away from us. For good people, what is removed and apparently taken away is everything that disagrees and conflicts, with the result that they are admitted to their love. It is much the same for evil people, except that what is taken away from them is everything true, while for good people*

everything false is taken away. Either way, the result is that ultimately everyone becomes his or her own love. (Swedenborg, Emanuel, *Heaven and Hell* (1758), #479, translated by G. F. Dole, 2000)

To generate a spiritual body that is able to subsist in the harmonic fields of Heaven, we must live in the world in accordance with Love, Wisdom and Use. Conscience connects us with the Love of Heaven, rationality with its Truth and usefulness with it Power. As we act in the world in accordance with our true values and loving principles, we collapse the wave-function of our being and its waves are able to interfere constructively with the waves of the universe and return to us as Love. This is how our spiritual body progressively grows and matures.

After digesting all the knowledge in this book, we can readily conclude that It is impossible to experience a joyful and meaningful life without having a harmonious relationship with God and other beings. Thus, human beings need religion as much as they require science. Throughout the ages, many scholars have attempted to reconcile science and religion. However, due to the spiritual fall of mankind, such a harmonization has never been realized. Through the course of history, scientists have contended that science is a domain of objective knowledge derived from impartial observation and facts while religion and spirituality are largely based on subjective beliefs and mystical revelations. As a consequence, these two disciplines should always be kept apart. Nonetheless, if a New Age of spiritual enlightenment is to unfold, we can no more separate science from religion than we can isolate man's intellect from his emotions. We can no more split religion and science than we can separate God from His creation. In the *New Jerusalem*, science and religion will be successfully reconciled and harmonized.

There is a story in the New Testament, which has largely been misinterpreted, that concerns the relationship between science and religion. The law of Moses required that every adult should pay a tax of half a shekel to support the temple. In Capernaum, when Jesus is asked to pay the tax, He says to Peter: "...go thou to the sea, and cast a hook, and take up the fish that first cometh up; and when thou hast opened his mouth, thou shalt find a shekel: that take, and give unto them for me and thee." Without *the science of correspondences*, which Swedenborg rediscovered, we would never know what this really means. Fish correspond to the sciences and every branch of science pays tribute to spirituality or religion because science and religion are connected in Reality. When we investigate the principles of science, we find that they arise from the spiritual principles of religion.

To reconcile science and religion is in effect to reconcile matter and spirit, the finite and the Infinite. Long before he had conscious access to spiritual realities, Swedenborg had pondered this question for many years. How could the Infinite One generate beings with a distinct self that is finite? And, moreover, how could these separate selves be conjoined with God without infringing upon the holiness of God's Infinite Reality? Swedenborg intuitively recognized that if he were able to solve this problem that all other quandaries that arise in science, philosophy and theology would be equally resolved. The solution to this eternal problem enabled Swedenborg to elaborate a new paradigm of the universe that reconciles science and religion:

> It seems as though what is infinite cannot be united to what is finite because there is no ratio between the infinite and the finite and because the finite cannot contain the infinite. There are two reasons, though, why there can be a union. The first is that the Infinite One created everything from himself; and the second is that the Infinite One cannot focus on anything in finite beings except what is infinite from him. This can seem to finite beings as though it were within them; and this provides a ratio between what is finite and what is infinite. The ratio does not come from anything finite but from the Infinite One within it. In this way, too, the finite can contain the infinite. What does this is not the finite being in and of itself, but the finite being in its apparent autonomy, derived from the One who is intrinsically infinite. (Swedenborg, Emanuel, *Divine Providence* (1764), #54, translated by G. F. Dole, 2003)

> GOD, WHO IS INFINITE, the Divine Esse, the I Am, is substance in Itself, and as the Infinite and the only substance. He is everywhere. There is no place where He is not. Therefore the universe and all the finite or bounded things thereof are brought forth in Him. The universe is finited only in the Infinite. Hence there exists an apparent vacuum which still is not a vacuum; for an interstitial nothing is not possible.

What appears empty is filled by the living Substance in Itself the Divine which Is. Thus in God we live, and move and have our being.

God wills to create finite, bounded, recipient forms, individuals, which He can both infill, and act upon. God, by the predicates of His living Esse, could not bring those recipient individuals into existence by fiat. But He could form them from small discrete particles of substance, or substantial, previously produced.

What is the source of these substantials, these minimal, first finited particles of substances, these primordial substantials from which God creates His universe? Since their creation by fiat, or from nothing, is precluded, therefore the Infinite, the living expanse, Substance in Itself, must be the Source and Origin of these minima of substance, of these primordial leasts, which are to act as the seeds and primitives of creation. There is no other substance from which recipient forms may be created.

God, the Infinite Esse, must needs give of His own substance to frame creation. This is the sacramental gift, as of His flesh, to be the bread and the flesh of His creatures.

The primitive substantials of creation must be formed from the substance of the Infinite Esse, God must give portions of His own substance to be the substantia prima from which He creates all things. God, therefore, must first finite His Infinity as a preparation for a universe.

The first finiting of Infinity, is, according to Swe-
denborg, the production of minimal and simplest
points of circulospiral motion, that is, the production
of vortex rings, small as points, in the Substance of
the Infinite. The interior conatus to circulation of
these vortex points is circulo-spiral; so that the whole
point is not only in a vortex flow, but also gyres con-
tinually around its own axis.

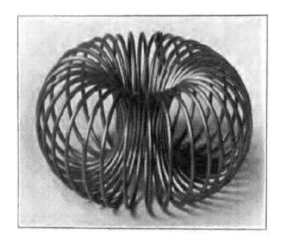

Fig. 12. 1. Vortex Ring

(Illustrating the perpetually spiral form and interior flux-
ion of finites.) From Beekman, Lillian G., *An Outline of*
Swedenborg's Cosmology, Academy Book Room, Bryn
Athyn, PA., 1907.

So long as the vortex flow of these minimal rings is continued and sustained by the will of God, they continue to exist as entities in the Substance of the Infinite; they continue in one aspect distinct and bounded, enclosed and limited; that is, the circling motion of their flow is a first delineation of finiting.

These simple minimal vortices were existent in the Infinite before any finite or concrete entity had existence. They are to be called the medium between the Infinite and the finite. They are not only the primitives of the first substantial or composites of creation, but they are its force and life. They are immediately Divine and superlatively perfect. In them are supremely involved the ends of the universe, its human result, and the providence of the future.

Moreover, the perpetually reflexive flow of these vortex points, these primitives and simples of finition, involves something deeper, more living still. In them is present in very figure and embodiment the image which manifests the inmost action of love, of love as a substance. For all love tends to return as a circle to the source from which it came. And love exists as a substance in God the Creator. There is thus a conatus in each thing of creation to return to its source. Therefore the primitive force in a simple is most perfectly adaptable and modifiable along all human building lines; for the Infinite is capable of varying it in infinite ways. (Beekman, Lillian G., An Outline of Swedenborg's Cosmology, Academy Book Room, Bryn Athyn, PA., 1907.)

The image in figure 12.1 was produced in 1902 and it is a representation of Swedenborg's ultimate particles that reconcile the finite and infinite. Today, it is becoming increasingly evident that the torus or vortex is prevalent in the essential structure of the universe. For example, Arthur M. Young predicted that the universe must be toroidal and Roger Penrose theorized that the fundamental particles of the universe are twistors. But, more than 200 years ago, Swedenborg already envisioned the form of these fundamental particles.

Swedenborg's amazing discovery is that the fundamental energy of the universe is Divine Love. And this energy exists in God. Love must necessarily be vortical because it is the only self-existent energy in the universe. Hence, Love must perpetually return into itself like a living and dynamic vortex. In this book, we have shown that, mathematically, the vortices of Love that Swedenborg refers to are represented by quaternions, octonions, sedenions and hypernumbers in mathematical or conceptual space. And their relationships, actions and interactions describe the harmonic structure of Divine Love or God's energy. Truth is the organization or form of Love. This form must be analogous to the human form because the universe is generated as a chaotic fractal and the human form is the culmination of billions of years of biological evolution. Human beings are able to reciprocate Love to their Creator. This is the whole meaning and purpose of creation:

> ....the purpose for which the world was made, lies in the highest or first Degree of the Divine Nature, in

the Divine Love. Love by its very nature demands an object. That object must be another than self, else the love of it would be self-love. Love, then, in order to exist, must create another than itself. This other that Love creates must not only be wholly other than its creative source, must feel itself to be absolutely apart and distinct from it, but it must be able to reciprocate this love, to love in return. For it is only in reciprocation that love is satisfied, that the end of love is attained.   (Sewall, Frank, *The New Metaphysics*, James Speirs, London, 1888.)

Since the whole universe was generated from Divine Love, we are able to be conjoined with God and others by Love. But, by returning to God and Heaven from the material world, we acquire and develop a self that is completely distinct from God. By freely reciprocating Love from this natural self, God is sure that our Love for Him and others is real, true and genuine. And, although all angels who are presently in Heaven are loving and unselfish, they still possess this separate, distinct and unique self which they obtained from their existence on Earth.

God generates the universe as a reflected image of Himself. The mirror which reflects this image is matter or Earth. And the perfect reflection or image of God is a Heaven of angels from the human race. Through Chaos theory and fractal geometry, we are also able to understand where evil originated. It was a consequence of freewill in man. Man freely descended into the knowledge of good and evil to exercise his spiritual freedom. Nevertheless, order is continually restored through the fractal generator and attractor of Love and every loving human being is eventually raised into Heaven.

The universe is a beautiful work art because it is freely generated by the infinitely complex and harmonically organized fractal generator of Divine Love. But what makes a work of art beautiful? Human works of art tend to evoke real feelings and true thoughts because they accurately portray reality. A beautiful painting consists of a diversity of forms, contrasts and colors but all these elements must be organized coherently. A beautiful symphony is comprised of a variety of musical chords but these chords must be linked harmonically. Drama and conflict are produced from the tension between light and shade, consonance and dissonance, order and disorder. But dissonance is ultimately resolved in consonance. Edwin Babitt understood this delicate balance between Unity and Diversity when he wrote:

...Unity is universal through all matter and mind, and is the expression of wholeness, oneness, centralization and organization.

Diversity is a universal law of nature, and exemplifies freedom, life, individuality, infinity, etc.

Harmony consists in the equal balance of Unity and Diversity, and this harmony is increased in exquisiteness in proportion to the number of these parts of Unity and Diversity. (Babbitt, Edwin D., *The Principles of Light and Color*, Babbitt & Co.,New York, 1878)

Like music, dance is an art form; it is an expression of human aesthetic movement. These graceful gestures translate human feelings into physical motion. Dancers can also tell a story as in the intricate choreography of a ballet (Fig. 12.2). Such a ballet is usually set to music. Like a play, these ballet performances may consist of several acts which unfold dramatically. The motions in dance and music convey emotions to our heart by correspondence because feelings of Love are harmonic e-motions. The harmonic motion of galaxies, stars, planets and moons is also a celestial dance because all beings in the universe are returning to Love.

Fig. 12.2. A Ballet Scene from Don Quixote

Michelangelo Buonarotti is one of the most famous artist, sculptor, architect and painter in the world. His works reflect beauty because they embody painstaking detail in their forms and colors. And yet, despite such precision, it only took him four years to complete the Sistine chapel ceiling which contains more than 300 figures of the

Bible. Among his many talents, he had an expertise in human anatomy. Moreover, when we analyze his painting of *The Creation of Adam*, we realize that he must have known some secrets from Heaven. In figure 12.3, we can see that God created Adam in His own image from the conceptual mind of Heaven.

Fig. 12.3. Creation of Adam (Michelangelo)
and Human Brain

Architectural works are a product of science and art. A successful building must not only be a beautiful and harmonious work of art; it must also be a useful and functional work of geometry, science and technology. Many temples on earth incorporate sacred geometry in their construction because these buildings were designed to reflect the harmonic proportions of Heaven. We know that the Great Pyramid of Giza was designed in accordance with the Golden Ratio and the whole pyramid complex is aligned with the stars of the Orion belt. However, many of us may not know that the Egyptian temple of Luxor was modeled according to the human structure and consciousness (Fig. 12.4). In his book, *The Temple in Man*, R. A. Schwaller de Lubicz, came to this conclusion:

The Temple of Luxor is indisputably devoted to the Human Microcosm. This consecration is not merely a simple attribution: the entire temple becomes a book explaining the secret functions of the organs and nerve centers. (Schwaller de Lubicz. R. A., *The Temple of Man*, 1949)

Fig. 12.4. Plan of the Temple of Luxor

When we know that Heaven is in the human form and that man embeds the Truth and Love of Heaven within the conceptual spaces of his mind and heart, this finding does not seem so surprising.

Cathedrals on earth also tend to be beautiful because they are an expression of the architect and artisans' love of God. The Basilica Sagrada Familia (Church of the Holy Family) in Barcelona Spain is a building that was conceived and started by the Spanish architect Antoni Gaudi in 1882 (Fig. 12.5). It is so complex that it is still under construction today, 134 years later. According to the latest estimates, work on this cathedral should be completed around 2032. The details in this sacred building are as intricate as the branches, leaves and flowers of a tree or the complex parts of the human form. But all these fractal details converge into one harmonic and coherent structure.

Fig. 12.5. The Sagrada Familia, Barcelona, Spain

The human structure is also a beautiful and useful work of art and science because it is material, biological, mental and spiritual. The trillions of organic cells in the human body interact harmonically to keep the human structure coherent, alive and functioning. And these cells are in correspondence with harmonic vortices of mind and will. Heaven and earth are also harmonically organized according to the human form and the Golden Ratio. Swedenborg discovered that art and architecture in Heaven are a projection of the harmonic structure of Love and Truth present in the hearts and minds of angels:

I have seen palaces in heaven of such magnificence as cannot be described. Above they glittered as if made of pure gold, and below as if made of precious stones, some more splendid than others. It was the same within. Both words and knowledge are inadequate to describe the decorations that adorned the rooms. On the side looking to the south there were parks, where, too, everything shone, in some places the leaves glistening as if made of silver, and fruit as if made of gold; while the flowers in their beds formed rainbows with their colors. Beyond the borders, where the view terminated, were seen other palaces. Such is the architecture of heaven that you would say that art there is in its art; and no wonder, because the art itself is from heaven. The angels said that such things and innumerable others still more perfect are presented before their eyes by the Lord; and yet these things are more pleasing to their minds than to their eyes, because in everyone of them they see a correspondence, and through the correspondences what is Divine. (Swedenborg, Emanuel, *Heaven and Hell* (1758), #185, translated by John C. Ager, 1900.)

Like many works of literature, the Bible or Word of God is a dramatic story. An interesting, suspenseful and dramatic work of literature consists of a particular setting, many characters, an interesting plot and a satisfying ending. A drama essentially consists of five acts: *exposition, rising action, climax, falling action,* and *denouement.* The first act or *exposition* introduces the setting, the characters and their background. The second act or *rising action* builds up the story through many events toward the climax. The third act or *climax* is the period of maximum conflict, tension and distress. The fourth act or *falling action* is where the action or battle between the protagonist and antagonist occurs. Finally, the fifth act or *denouement* is where conflict is resolved. A tragedy ends in catastrophe or the death of some characters, as in Romeo and Juliette. In Dante's *Divine Comedy,* Dante travels through hell, purgatory and paradise. This story is believed by many to be a parable of the journey of the human soul.

The story of the universe must be the ultimate work of art; it is a love story between God and humanity. The first act introduces the characters of this drama in the Garden of Eden or a state of original human innocence and goodness. The Adamic people were in harmonic relationship with each other and God. The second act is the fall of the Adamic race into the knowledge of good and evil, culmi-

nating in a spiritual flood and the Noachian race. The
Noachian Church also degrades and is devastated. In the
the third act, the Israelitish Church is born and raised. The
age of the Israelites ends in a climax where the Word is
completely materialized. The fourth act consists of the incarnation of Divine Truth on Earth and a battle between
Good and evil, Truth and falsehood, Heaven and hell. This
act peaks with the crucifixion, glorification, resurrection
and ascension of Jesus the Messiah. But through the passage of 2000 years, the Christian Church also becomes
corrupted, degraded and devastated. The fifth and final
act will be the revelation of the spiritual meaning of the
Word and the establishment of the *New Jerusalem* where
humanity will be reconciled with God.

If the universe were uniquely governed by Law, it
would be as meaningless, monotonous and uninteresting
as the mechanism of a clock. If it were solely the result of
Freedom and uncertainty, it would ultimately degenerate
into complete disorder and absurdity. The universe is a
dramatic, interesting and beautiful work of art because it
is a chaotic fractal. And a chaotic fractal is able to reconcile Freedom and Law, Chaos and Order, Diversity and
Unity. The whole universe is propelled and motivated by
Love. And every being is free to express and realize this
Love in his own unique and distinct way. Hence, disorder
may continue to increase. However, on every level, when
disorder reaches its maximum, the strange attractor of
Love restores Order. The underlying laws of the universe
are a manifestation of Divine Order or Truth. Although all
humans are free to either reciprocate or reject Love, God
knows and influences the form of the future: He knows

that the future state of the universe is a Heaven of angels from the human race. And God is present with us in the conceptual spaces or Heavens of our mind:

The heavens declare the glory of God;
And the firmament showeth his handiwork.
Day unto day uttereth speech,
And night unto night showeth knowledge.
There is no speech nor language;
Their voice is not heard.
Their line is gone out through all the earth,
And their words to the end of the world.
In them hath he set a tabernacle for the sun,
Which is as a bridegroom coming out of his chamber,
And rejoiceth as a strong man to run his course.
His going forth is from the end of the heavens,
And his circuit unto the ends of it;
And there is nothing hid from the heat thereof.

                                        Psalm 19

We have seen that the essence of God is harmony. And all harmony is a reconciliation between Diversity and Unity, Freedom and Law, Order and Chaos. All worlds and beings were generated through harmony and return to Heaven and God through harmony. All elementary particles are harmonic conjugates. Space and matter are harmonic conjugates. Electricity and magnetism are harmonic conjugates. Positive charge and negative discharge are harmonic conjugates. Radiation and gravitation are harmonic conjugates. Galaxies, stars and planets rotate, revolve and precess in accordance with the harmonic order of Love. Only atoms that are in harmony combine to form harmonic molecular compounds. DNA is the most complex and harmonic molecule in the molecular world.

All creatures return to Love by seeking, finding and uniting with their harmonic conjugate. All creatures procreate through harmony. Male and female are harmonic conjugates. Plants procreate through pollination and fertilization. Every animal seeks its harmonic conjugate. Every human being returns to Love by seeking, finding and marrying his or her harmonic conjugate. The human male represents Wisdom and the human female corresponds to Love. The marriage of a human male and a human female is sacred because it corresponds to the marriage of Wisdom and Love in God. A man and a woman procreate through *conjugial*[2] Love. Their sons and daughters correspond to new Truths and Goods that have the potential to increase the harmony of Love in Heaven.

Heaven and Earth are harmonic conjugates. The harmony of all those human beings who love God and obey the laws of Heaven is the *Universal Church*. The Lord is the bridegroom and the Church is the bride. The conjunction of the Lord with the Church and the reciprocal conjunction of the Church with the Lord is called a *marriage*. Man receives Truth and Good by influx from God. When Truth

---

2   Swedenborg specifically used the word *conjugial* instead of the more common word *conjugal* in order to emphasize the difference between a sexual relationship that is in correspondence with the spiritual principles of Heaven and one that is only the result of sexual lust. It also may be a meaningful coincidence that "i" or $\sqrt{-1}$ is a quaternion in conceptual or spiritual space.

and Good are harmonically conjoined, Heaven is formed
by the Lord in man:

*It is further true that all true harmony in universal
realms derives its beauty from the fact that it is not
beautiful by itself, but from others, and thus from
the beauty of all, this being the case with all harmonies and the individual one. If, therefore, a single
harmony did not regard the other, but itself, nothing
harmonious would ever result.*

*Hence it can be known that every man is allotted
his own province, and that there is indefinite variety
and harmony of all, as there is with each and all
things in man. Thus it is that the whole is composed
of the harmony of the varieties, and that it has been
foreseen and provided that all who inherit heaven
may be parts of this Grand Man, thus be in the Lord.
Also, that heaven can never be closed even to eternity, for the more there are in a society, and the more
societies there are, so much the better, the more
blessed, and the stronger they are.* (Swedenborg,
Emanuel, *Spiritual Experiences* (1800), #1364, #1837,
translated by D. Odhner, 1998)

*Such being the nature of heaven, no angel or spir-
it can have any life unless he is in some society, and
thereby in a harmony of many. A society is nothing
but a harmony of many, for no one has any life separate from the life of others. Indeed no angel, or spirit,
or society can have any life (that is, be affected by
good, exercise will, be affected by truth, or think),*

unless there is a conjunction thereof through many of his society with heaven and with the world of spirits. And it is the same with the human race: no man, no matter who and what he may be, can live (that is, be affected by good, exercise will, be affected by truth, or think), unless in like manner he is conjoined with heaven through the angels who are with him, and with the world of spirits, nay, with hell, through the spirits that are with him. For every man while living in the body is in some society of spirits and of angels, though entirely unaware of it. And if he were not conjoined with heaven and with the world of spirits through the society in which he is, he could not live a moment.

The case in this respect is the same as it is with the human body, any portion of which that is not conjoined with the rest by means of fibers and vessels, and thus by means of functions, is not a part of the body, but is instantly separated and rejected, as having no vitality. The very societies in and with which men have been during the life of the body, are shown them when they come into the other life. And when, after the life of the body, they come into their society, they come into their veriest life which they had in the body, and from this life begin a new life; and so according to their life which they have lived in the body they either go down into hell, or are raised up into heaven. (Swedenborg, Emanuel, *Arcana Coelestia* (1749-56), #687, translated by John F. Potts, 1905.)

We started this book with mathematics and numbers. And we discovered that Irrational and Transcendental numbers are dynamic, alive, infinitely rational and fractal. In fact, these numbers are a representation of what is taking place within the conceptual space of our mind. Numbers are in effect describing the Divine order or Truth of our rational mind and our relationship with the Infinite One or God. The relationship and interaction of e, π, i, φ, quaternions, octonions and sedenions describe the fractal generator and strange attractor of Divine Love. The spinning and precessing of quaternions is a mathematical, geometrical and conceptual representation of the involution/evolution or harmonic e-motion of Love. The universe is perpetually generated, maintained and restored by the real, eternal and living energy of Love. Our own freewill is a gift of God's Divine Energy. And we can only enter God's Heavenly Kingdom by reciprocating this Love consciously, freely and willingly. The more angels Heaven contains, the more perfectly it reflects the image of God:

> *The perfection of heaven increases according to its numbers, is evident from its form, according to which its associations are disposed in order, and its communications flow, for it is the most perfect of all; and in proportion to the increase of numbers in that most perfect form, there is given a direction and consent of more and more to unity, and therefore a closer and a more unanimous conjunction; the consent and the conjunction derived from it increase from numbers, for everything is there inserted as a mediate relation between two or more, and what is*

inserted confirms and conjoins. The form of heaven is like the form of the human mind, the perfection of which increases according to the increase of truth and good, from whence are its intelligence and wisdom.

The form of the human mind, which is in heavenly wisdom and intelligence, is like the form of heaven, because the mind is the least image of that form; hence it is, that on all sides there is a communication of the thoughts and affections of good and truth in such men, and in angels, with surrounding societies of heaven; and an extension according to the increase of wisdom, and thus according to the plurality of the knowledges of truth implanted in the intellect and according to the abundance of the affections of good implanted in the will; and therefore in the mind, for the mind consists of the intellect and the will. The human and angelic mind is such that it may be infilled to eternity, and as it is infilled, so it is perfected; and this is especially the case, when man is led by the Lord, for he is then introduced into genuine truths, which are implanted in his intellect, and into genuine goods, which are implanted in his will, for the Lord then disposes all things of such a mind into the form of heaven, until at length it is a heaven in the least form.

From this comparison, which is a true parallel, it is evident, that the increasing number of the angels perfects heaven. Moreover, every form consists of various parts; a form which does not consist of vari-

ous parts, is not a form, for it has no quality, and no changes of state; the quality of every form results from the arrangement of various things within it, from their mutual relation, and from their consent to unity, from which every form is considered as one; such a form, in proportion to the multitude of the various things arranged within it, is the more perfect, for every one of them, as was said above, confirms, corroborates, conjoins, and so perfects. (Swedenborg, Emanuel, *The last Judgment* (1758), #12, translated by John Whitehead, 1892.)

For ages, man has sought and failed to find God. Scientists have sought Him in the harmonic order of the planets or the symmetry of elementary particles. Philosophers and mathematicians have sought Him in the conceptual spaces of their mind. Artists have sought Him in the beauty and life of natural and conceptual forms. Mothers and fathers have sought Him in the innocent face of their child. Finally, due to the disorder in the world, many have given up hope of ever finding God. However, when we discover that Love is the underlying Reality of the universe and that it is God's energy, we realize that God is very close to us. And, if disorder were not tolerated in the world, there would be no freedom, no change and no evolution. Human beings would be like robots. The only reason the universe is purposeful and meaningful is because Love can only be reciprocated freely and willingly. And this means that humans are free to abuse their gift of freewill and generate disorder within their mind as well as in the world. Yet, Divine Justice is eternally realized because the omnipresent attractor of Love restores harmony everywhere.

When we witness what continues to unfold in the world today, all the greed, fear and hatred that still persists within man's heart, the conflicts between nations, the violence, crimes and wars that still afflict many cities on earth, it is difficult to imagine a world motivated by Love. However, when human beings will have finally understood that Earth is simply a place where new human souls are generated and prepared for the real life of Heaven, they will be united by a common understanding of Truth and mutual feelings of Love. In the *New Jerusalem*, we should expect that the heart of every human being will be healed and reconciled with God by Love, and everyone will have the Truth written upon his own heart:

> *But this is the covenant that I will make with the house of Israel after those days, says YHVH: I will put my law in their inward parts, and in their heart will I write it; and I will be their God, and they shall be my people: and they shall teach no more everyone their neighbor, and every man his brother, saying, Know YHVH; for they shall all know me, from the least of them to the greatest of them, says YHVH: for I will forgive their iniquity, and their sin will I remember no more.* Jeremiah 31

REFERENCES

Adams, George and Whicher, Olive, *The Plant Between Sun and Earth*, Shambhala, Boulder, Colorado, 1982.

Babbitt, Edwin D., *The Principles of Light and Color*, Babbitt & Co., New York, 1878.

Baker, Gregory L., *Religion and Science: From Swedenborg to Chaotic Dynamics*, The Solomon Press, Publishers, New York, 1992.

Bayley, Jonathan, *From Egypt to Canaan*, New Church Press, London, 1869.

Bayley, Jonathan, *The Divine Wisdom of the Word of God*, James Speirs, London, 1892.

Bayley, Jonathan, *The Divine Word Opened*, William White, London, 1858.

Beekman, Lillian G., *An Outline of Swedenborg's Cosmology*, Academy Book Room, Bryn Athyn, PA., 1907.

Blackwood, John, *Geometry of Nature*, Floris Books, Edinburgh, UK, 2012.

Blattman, Georg, *The Sun: The Ancient Mysteries and a New Physics*, Floris Books, Edinburgh, UK, 1985.

Bohm, David and F. David Peat, *Science, Order and Creativity*, Bantam Books, New York, 1987.

Briggs, John, *Fractals, The Pattern of Chaos*, Simon & Schuster, New York, 1992.

Briggs, John and F. David Peat, *Looking Glass Universe*, Simon & Schuster, New York, 1984.

Briggs, John and F. David Peat, *Seven Life Lessons of Chaos*, Harper Collins Publishers, New York, 1999.

Briggs, John and F. David Peat, *Turbulent Mirror*, Harper & Rowe Publishers, New York, 1989.

Bruce, William, *Commentary on The Gospel According to St. John*, The Missionary Society of the New Church, London, 1870.

Bruce, William, *Commentary on The Gospel according to St. Matthew* , London, 1867.

Burger, Bruce, *Esoteric Anatomy*, North Atlantic Books Berkely, California, 1998.

De Charms, George, *Structural Harmony of the Old and New Testaments*, New Church Life, 1921.

De Charms, George, *Suggested Harmony of the Old and New Testaments*, New Church Life, 1963.

Edwards, Lawrence, *Projective Geometry*, Rudolf Steiner Institute, Phoenixville, Pennsylvania, 1985.

Edwards, Lawrence, *The Vortex of Life*, Floris Books, Edinburgh, 1993.

Evans, Warren Felt, *The New Age and its Messenger*, T.H. Carter & Co., Boston, 1864.

French, Thomas, *The New Jerusalem, Vital Questions briefly answered,* 1900.

Haish, Bernard, *The God Theory*, Weiser Books, San Francisco, CA, 2009.

Haish, Bernard, *The Purpose-Guided Universe*, New Page Books, Franklin Lakes, NJ, 2010.

Haller, John, S. Jr., *Swedenborg, Mesmer and the Mind/Body Connection*, Swedenborg Foundation Press, West Chester, Pennsylvania, 2010.

Hoeck, Louis G., *The Tree of Life*, The American New Church Tract and Publication Society, Philadelphia, Pa. 1940.

Johnson Jr., Willie, *The Gyroscopic Force Theory*, Lulu Books, June 30, 2011.

Johnson Jr., Willie, *Po Pi Phi Psi: The ijk's of Vortex Mathematics*, Lulu Books, July 20, 2013.

Johnson Jr., Willie, *The Sagitta Key*, Lulu Books, August 30, 2014.

Jonsson, Inge, *Visionary Scientist, The Effects of Science and Philosophy on Swedenborg's Cosmology*, Swedenborg Foundation Publishers, West Chester Pennsylvania. 1999.

Laszlo, Ervin, *Science and the Akashic Field*, Inner Traditions, Rochester Vermont, 2004.

Madley, Edward, *The Science of Correspondences Elucidated*, Swedenborg Publishing Association, 1888.

Mitchell, Edward Craig, *Scripture Symbolism*, William H. Alden, Philadelphia, 1904.

Mitchell, Edward Craig, *The Parables of the New Testament Spiritually Explained*, William H. Alden, Philadelphia, 1888.

Mitchell, Edward Craig, *The Parables of the Old Testament Explained*, William H. Alden, Philadelphia, 1903.

Odhner, C. T., *Correspondences of Canaan*, Academy Book Room, Bryn Athyn, PA, 1911.

Odhner, C. Th., *The Correspondences of Egypt*, Academy Book Room, Bryn Athyn, Pa., 1914.

Odhner, C. Th., *The Golden Age*, Academy Book Room, Bryn Athyn, Pa., 1913.

Ogilvy, Stanley C., *Excursions in Geometry*, Dover Publications Inc., New York, 1969.

Ouspensky, P. D., *A New Model of the Universe*, Vintage, New York, 1971.

Ouspensky, P. D., *In Search of the Miraculous*, Harcourt-Brace Inc., New York, 1949.

Ouspensky, P. D., *The Psychology of Man's Possible Evolution*, Vintage Books, New York, 1950.

Peat, David, F., *Blackfoot Physics*, Weiser Books, Boston

MA/York Beach ME, 2005.

Peat, David, F., *The Philosopher's Stone*, Bantam Books, New York, 1991.

Peat, David, F., *Superstrings and the Search for The Theory of Everything*, Contemporary Books, Chicago Illinois, 1988.

Peat, David, F., *Synchronicity: The Bridge between Matter and Mind*, Bantam Books, New York, 1988.

Penrose, Roger, *The Road to Reality*, Vintage Books, London, 2005.

Russell, Walter, *The Secret of Light*, University of Science and Philosophy, Waynesboro, Virginia, 1947.

Russell, Walter, *The Message of the Divine Illiad, Vol. I & II*, University of Science and Philosophy, Waynesboro, Virginia, 1948-9.

Schwenk, Theodor, *Sensitive Chaos*, Rudolf Steiner Press, Forest Row, East Sussex, UK, 1965.

Seifer, Marc, *Transcending the Speed of Light*, Inner Traditions, Rochester, Vermont, 2008.

Sewall, Frank, *The Angel of the State*, E. A. Whiston, Boston, 1896.

Sewall, Frank, *Swedenborg and the Sapientia Angelica*, Constable & co. ltd, London, 1910.

Sewall, Frank, *The New Ethics*, G. P. Putnam's Sons, New York, 1881.

Sewall, Frank, *The New Metaphysics*, James Speirs, London, 1888.

Steiner, Rudolph, *The Fourth Dimension*, Anthroposophic Press, Great Barrington, Massachusetts, 2000.

Swedenborg, Emanuel,

  Arcana Coelestia (1749-56), translated by John F. Potts, 1905.

  Apocalypse Explained (1757-9), translated by John Whitehead, 1911.

Apocalypse Revealed (1766), translated by John Whitehead, 1912.

Conjugial Love (1768) , translated by Samuel H. Warren and Louis H. Tafel, 1915

Coronis (1771), translated by John Whitehead, 1914.

De Verbo (1762), translated by John Whitehead, 1914.

Heaven and Hell (1758), translated by John C. Ager, 1900.

Divine Providence (1764), translated by William Frederic Wunsch, 1851.

Divine Love and Wisdom (1763), translated by John C. Ager, 1890.

Doctrine of the Lord (1763), translated by John C. Ager, 1904.

Doctrine of Sacred Scripture (1763) translated by John F. Potts, 1904.

Heaven and Hell (1758) translated by John C. Ager, 1900.

An Hierogryphic Key to Natural and Spiritual Mysteries, by Way of Representations and Correspondences, translated by R. Hindmarsh, 1792.

New Jerusalem and its Heavenly Doctrines (1758), translated by John Whitehead, 1892.

The Principia (1734), translated by James R. Randell and Isaiah Tansley, 1912.

Rational Psychology (1743) translated by Frank Sewall, 1849.

Spiritual Diary (1747-65) translated by Bush, Smithson and Buss, 1883-9.

Spiritual Experiences (1745-65) translated by C. Odhner, 1788.

True Christian Religion (1771), translated by John Whitehead, 1906.

The White Horse (1758), translated by John Whitehead, 1892.

Sills, Franklin, *The Polarity Process*, North Atlantic Books, Berkeley, California, 2002.

Sylvia, Edward S., *Proving God*, Staircase Press, Troy, IL, 2009.

Thomas, Nick, C., *Space and Counterspace*, Floris Books, Edinburgh, UK, 2008.

Thompson, Ian J., *Starting Science from God*, Eagle Pearl Press, Pleasanton, California, 2011.

Whicher, Olive, *The Heart of the Matter*, Temple Lodge London, 1997.

Whicher, Olive, *Projective Geometry*, Rudolf Steiner Press, London, 1971.

Whicher, Olive, *Sunspace*, Rudolf Steiner Press, London, 1989.

Worcester, John, *Correspondences of the Bible, The Animals*, Lockwood, Brooks, and co., London, 1875.

Worcester, John, *Correspondences of the Bible, The Plants, The Minerals and The Atmospheres*, Massachusetts New Church Union, Boston, 1930.

Worcester, John, *Physiological Correspondences*, Massachusetts New Church Union, Boston, 1931.

Worcester, William L., *On Holy Ground*, J. B. Lippincott Company, New York and London, 1904.

Worcester, William L. *The Language of Parable*, New York, 1892.

Young, Arthur M., *Mathematics, Physics and Reality*, Robert Briggs Associates, Lake Oswego, Oregon, 1990.

Young, Arthur M.,*The Geometry of Meaning*, Robert Briggs Associates, Mill Valley, Ca., 1976.

Young, Arthur M., *The Reflexive Universe*, Robert Briggs Associates, Lake Oswego, Oregon, 1976.

Zajonc, Arthur, *Catching the Light: The Entwined History of Light and Mind*, Bantam Press, London, 1993.

Credits

Front Cover. Chaotic Beauty, Courtesy of NASA, Image Credit: NASA/JPL-Caltech/R. A. Gutermuth (Harvard-Smithsonian CfA)

Fig. 1.22, *Jacob and Esau and the Mess of Pottage,* Painting by Jan Victors, 1652.

Fig. 2.6, Computer Simulation of Large Scale Galaxy Clusters, Joerg Colberg, Virgo Simulations: Jenkins et al, 1998 Astrophysical Journal, 499, 20-40.

Fig. 3.4, *The Garden of Eden*, painting by Jacopo Bassano (1510-1592).

Fig. 4.2, Planets of the Solar System, courtesy of NASA.

Fig. 9.1, Heaven, from *The Empyrean (highest heaven),* from the illustrations to The Divine Comedy by Gustave Doré, 19th century.

Page 261, *The Woman Clothed with the Sun Fleeth from the Persecution of the Dragon,* Benjamin West, 1797.

Fig 10.3, The Atom with its Spirals and its Influx and Efflux Ethers. From Babbitt, Edwin D., *The Principles of Light and Color*, Babbitt & Co., New York, 1878.

Fig. 10.5, Plexi of Nervous System, from C. W. Leadbeater, *The Chakras*, 1927.

Fig. 12.3, The Creation of Adam, a fresco painted by Michelangelo, the work started at 1508 and finished 1512.

Made in the USA
Las Vegas, NV
21 November 2020